An Epic Odyssey

of

Madness

And

Mayhem

"An Epic Odyssey of Madness and Mayhem," by Carla Bastos. ISBN 978-1-951985-73-8 (softcover), 978-1-951985-74-5 (eBook).

Published 2020 by Virtualbookworm.com Publishing Inc., P.O. Box 9949, College Station, TX 77842, US. © 2020 Carla Bastos. All rights reserved. No part of this publication may be reproduced, stored in a retrieval system, or transmitted in any form or by any means, electronic, mechanical, recording or otherwise, without the prior written permission of Carla Bastos.

To Zendejas

Contents

The Odyssey of Humankind

A Little Grace

In keeping with the age-old problem of never having enough spit (much like Hooper as he was about to go down in the anti-shark cage), the boy licked his lips desperately, his eyes darting from one end of the field to the other in search of an escape. I winced. He looked maybe nine or ten. And not particularly happy.

"Really, all forty-five?" the woman said with a generous smile. The boy's mom had cornered her in one of the festival booths, insisting her son could name every American president in order. Like me, the woman probably doubted he could do it and, even if he could, she didn't quite get the point of it all. It wasn't as if she was a prep school headmistress or wielded any particular power to reward the kid's effort.

Did this lady just cart her son around trying to impress random disinterested people for sport? It was an art festival after all, and the woman was obviously a total stranger in a huge field full of people minding their own business just trying to take in some authentic southwestern creations. Where on earth did she think her son's presidential acumen fit in? *Please don't do this to your child,* I silently pleaded with her. But an unnatural fascination with why people do the things they do demanded I hang around to find out if she would. I'd lost interest in the collection of buffalo watercolors anyway.

Mercifully, the woman congratulated him for being such a smart young man but lamented she was running late and wouldn't have time to stick around for the full display of his brilliance.

I was relieved for the boy's sake that the woman showed such grace, and his mom hadn't chosen some mean-spirited loser with nothing better to do than humiliate a child. But I still didn't get it.

We all like to brag on our kids' and grandkids' exploits and accomplishments. Lord knows I've probably driven a few people to drink in my day, regaling them with stories of my granddaughters' awesomeness. Some folks feel a need to vicariously accomplish all sorts of things that they failed at in their youth. Those with a competitive (or slightly sick) bent insist that their kid outperform every classmate, teammate or neighbor, be it in sports or academics or just plain looking good. But, in some cases there seems to be more at play.

Is it just me, or do some parents want to pit their children against others much like I might pit my muscle car against yours? The problem with that whole dynamic is that the children then become, not unlike those muscle cars, mere objects. Things. Possessions. And mine are better than yours. Even when there's no one to compete with, folks are dragging their children around art festivals trying to prove to somebody, anybody, how exceptional they are.

It's a phenomenon that goes beyond just our kids. It's our pets, homes, wardrobes, relationships, jobs, our very lives. And it doesn't seem to be enough that all these things are good, or even great. They must be *better,* superior in some way.

While sitting at a round table with a dozen other women we'd never met, waiting for a Bible study to get underway, my friend and I were quietly discussing our recent travels. I'd been to Wimbledon that year and she to Brazil, and we hadn't really had a chance to talk since. We both loved travel and happened to mention other destinations on our respective bucket lists. Out of the blue, from across the table, one of the women interjected, *I'm glad I'm not so insecure that I have to escape from my life all the time.*

After recovering from shock and a momentary flirtation with inadequacy (*Was* I insecure???), I pretty quickly decided this chick was crazy and it would be best not to engage. But the incident spoke volumes.

I've done a bunch of very cool things. I have a wonderful son and daughter-in-law and a couple of amazing grandchildren. I'm pretty satisfied, and very gratified, with my life. But at no time have I ever felt a need to have a *better* life, or family, or things, than anyone else. In our society, I fear healthy competition has become a kind of weird, obsessive, jealousy that is very unhealthy and a huge waste of time.

One of the drawbacks to living in an affluent society is the inability to know what matters—even what matters to each of us as individuals. Our focus is on all the shiny things all around us, and how their owners acquired those shiny things. Have we stopped to ask ourselves if we even *want* that particular thing? Or if our children have even the slightest interest in what the Joneses' children are excelling at, or the many things we ourselves were unable to accomplish?

Life is short, and we might do well to be about living our own and not worrying about anyone else's. Contrary to popular belief, we really don't have to be faster, better or stronger. Like the wise victim of that young presidential scholar's mom, perhaps just congratulate one another and move on. Maybe even offer up a little grace.

* * *

Everything Lasts a Minute

Have you ever noticed how quickly things come and go? Experiences, feelings, fads and trends. Flavors of the month now last only a week, or even a day. Not that I have a problem with this, mind you, even though I'm old and can't keep up. No, I think it's a wonderful thing to live in a fast-paced age where there's so much to learn and we have the tools to access these exciting new things. My only question is whether we are actually …learning.

By definition, the act of learning must involve extrapolating and retaining facts or information or processes that can improve or correct past behaviors and errors. The key here is the retaining part. And, of course, distinguishing between a fad and a lesson.

During a conversation with a very sharp, well-informed colleague, I made what I thought was a brilliant, not to mention hilarious, pop culture reference to illustrate a point. Except it was from 1985 pop culture. Sure, it was all the rage at the time. But it held no lasting, informative value. I learned (and retained) this important lesson when my colleague looked at me as if I was from Mars and I began to feel a desperate need to check a mirror to be sure I hadn't inadvertently put on my red nose and clown shoes that morning. Old movie quotes and song lyrics may be great for my personal amusement or edification, but they'll do nothing to enhance society as a whole.

Today, it seems the tables have been turned. Everything's upside down. All the pop culture nonsense is just what the doctor ordered. It's what today's society loves, and it's what folks seem to hang on to and somehow deem important. These are the things that *should* only last a minute, but are hung on to for dear life, inciting endless (and mindless) online banter, heated arguments, accusations and hate.

Also quite common these days, something else that we tend to make last for as long as possible, is even the hint of a difficult or negative experience, even of one's own making, that might create an opportunity to grab a little attention. *Oh, that's nothing, let me tell you what happened to me…*

First of all, actions have consequences. So, if we've had to pay said consequences for our own actions, we would do well to learn the lesson and move on. Instead, if we don't feel we're getting sufficient sympathy or perhaps not everyone on the planet has yet heard, we just milk it for all it's worth.

Then there is the bad stuff that just happens, through no fault of our own. It's called life. Once again, move on. Let the insignificant things, and the things we cannot change, roll off—the things that are little more than entertainment or gossip or drama flooding social media, the things that will not make one iota of difference in the grand scheme of things. These non-issues are not worthy of more than a minute of our time.

So yes, we get to, and must, forget the stuff that doesn't matter. But there should be a law against forgetting the important stuff—maybe a periodic mandatory quiz or something.

Say, for example, members of the House and Senate stood on the Capitol steps following an unspeakable attack on our country, and broke into a spontaneous, rousing chorus of *God Bless America.* Wow, that would be something to remember. A lesson in camaraderie and bipartisanship.

Or, what if a phenomenon occurred in which a global pandemic could be quelled simply by populations wearing face coverings and staying a few feet apart until the threat subsided? Then the life lesson would indeed be to employ that remedy until the threat subsided, and not just for the minute until our patience was exhausted.

Or, perhaps a group of people who had never before in life considered the human condition of another group, was confronted by a series of horrific images crashing into their awareness and forcing them to face facts that were previously just too inconvenient to acknowledge. The former group links arms with the latter in at least an effort toward alliance, demanding change. Hard to imagine, sure, but such an awakening would certainly be a life lesson that must never be abandoned.

It's worth considering *why* we choose to give lasting attention to nonsense. Is it just more fun and entertaining? Are the weighty, consequential matters just too difficult? Have we become a society without hope, making indifference our only option? Or, are we just lazy and content and uninterested in learning anything of any consequence?

Pop culture was once an indulgence, largely concentrated among youth. For mature adults it was little more than an insignificant, occasional escape from serious thought and conversation. After all, it's not healthy to take ourselves too seriously. But, we're in trouble when pop culture becomes fodder for serious thought and conversation, among the population at large.

What must last more than a fleeting moment? Humankind has the wherewithal to determine true priorities, those all-important, history-defining matters that demand our tireless attention. Once we've made that determination, then it's time to engage. To fight the good fight, from a sincere heart rather than for a photo op or for our own selfish gain, not being distracted by the nonsense, and not stopping until we've thoroughly learned the lessons—and finished the race.

* * *

Without Whimsy

One explanation for many of our ills and woes today is clear and simple: something is missing.

The concept occurred to me while reading an article on the problem with the American diet. It seems we've become good at cutting out things that are bad for us, but sometimes we neglect to add certain essentials. No matter how much fat, sugar, fried foods or carbs we cut out, our health still suffers because important nutrients found in dark green leafy veggies, etc., are absent.

So, consider the human condition in the 21st century. The advances, discoveries and inventions we've made, the mountains we've climbed and challenges we've conquered were unimaginable just a few years ago. Technological advances have left many of us in the dust. We are closer than ever before to curing cancer. We can talk to people across the globe with our fingertips. We can choose and embrace "friends" online whom we'll never meet in person.

And yet...

We are miserable, paranoid and self-loathing. We are ignorant and small-minded, jealous and judgmental. We insult, attack, hate, and kill each other. We are lonely islands who resent the sharing of the ocean that surrounds us.

Even without taking into account politics, the economy, racial inequality, global warming or anything else we're passionate about; notwithstanding social status, job security, city vs. suburbs, east coast vs. west, whether a cause be of dire importance and urgency or just the latest fad; despite all the attention we assign to just trying to survive or, for those more fortunate or privileged, to winning against all odds and at anyone else's expense—the bottom line is still the same. In every circumstance there seems to be something missing. Something that may contribute to making or breaking an outcome.

We are a people, a society, and a world without whimsy. The mere refusal to lighten up is killing us. (Yes, there are a myriad of other issues that are the collective cause of all our woes, but it might behoove us to start with the easy ones.)

I've never been a joiner, but during the COVID-19 quarantine I was forced to interact with a couple of groups online, groups that I'd contributed to in an editorial capacity but to whom I had no particular allegiance. Only then did I fully realize the serious void that could only be filled by whimsy. Everyone in the group took themselves soooo seriously. As discussions heightened to nearly unbearable decibel levels (and sometimes devolved into little more than juvenile drama), time and time again I would find it necessary to extricate myself.

These are dreadful times to be sure, and we must passionately pursue justice, equality, and physical, mental and emotional health. But we must do so wisely. Whatever we devote our efforts to, whether fighting for our own rights or someone else's, we should prepare for the long haul. Life is a marathon, every aspect of it, and we simply cannot successfully go the distance if we don't remember the importance of balance.

Think of flight attendants' instructions to put the oxygen mask on ourselves before our children. Translation: We'll be of no help to anyone else if we haven't first taken care of self. An essential part of that care is whimsy—joy, humor, a little fantastical escape every now and again.

Mind you, by whimsy I don't mean the latest recreational trends, things that are cost-prohibitive for most people anyway. That would amount to little more than another source of stress—forcing ourselves to "have fun" doing something because someone on the internet said *everyone* is doing it.

No, by whimsy I'm thinking of a whole different kind of escape. Like the young man who posted footage of himself skipping through a field with reckless abandon, leaping and clicking his heels. The post included an unexpected explanation: *I frolicked for the first time today, bruh. Y'all ever frolic before? How come no one ever told me about this?*

Once his tweet went viral, he followed up with words of wisdom: *If you're having a bad day, just frolic. I promise, you'll feel better.*

Whimsy, people. Whimsy.

So, where do we begin? First things first. We can't fully embrace whimsy unless we also eliminate, at least temporarily, the aforementioned stress and angst of life today.

I submit for your consideration:

- Perhaps don't sign up for every membership, download every app, join every group or make every purchase that's dangled in front of you just because it's the latest trend (all the while knowing it will only plunge you deeper into debt, despair and anxiety).

- Think about not sharing every fleeting thought or moment of every day with everyone in the world on social media, knowing it will incite ridiculous, ugly, time-wasting debates.

- Stop worrying so much about what everyone thinks of you.

- Take a walk. Maybe do something quirky along the way, like sing out loud or practice your dance moves. (Although, if you're too embarrassed to frolic, I'm pretty sure you won't be dancing either.)

- Eat some ice cream, or some bread, or whatever else you've sworn off of.

- Watch a comedy—not a sarcastic, hateful one, but an old, real, pure, side-splitting classic.

You get the idea. Just stop taking yourself so seriously, at least once in a while.

Sure, it sounds almost too simple, and I just know there are people reading this and grumbling, *I don't have time for any friggin' whimsy.* But, please consider, we're in deep, uncharted waters these days, too often just making things up as we go. I contend that the only way to successfully navigate those waters is to add a little whimsy. It may be the consummate missing ingredient.

* * *

Old Cool

The couple must have been in their seventies, probably pushing eighty. I knew they lived near me because I'd seen them pretty often tooling around Albuquerque in their old red Mazda Miata, top down, sometimes him driving, sometimes her. She always wore aviator sunglasses while he sported a newsboy or Panama hat, occasionally even a Yankee cap. The license plate on the Miata was what I'd first noticed. *We Be Old.*

I knew right away that I wanted to be like them when I reached retirement. They always seemed so relaxed and content, such a devil-may-care demeanor. And after all, if you're gonna hang around until seniorhood, you may as well be a cool senior. These two were the embodiment of cool. Or so I thought.

I'd only seen them in the car, sometimes at a red light or slowly making their way through side streets, but often enough zipping down Paseo Del Norte at a rate of speed once reserved for the young. But one lazy Sunday afternoon I spotted the car in a parking lot. It was one of Albuquerque's quirky, out of the way, anti-Starbucks coffee shops, ever so fitting for my hero couple. I just had to know more, so I decided to stalk, I mean observe, them.

She sat in one of a pair of wingback chairs in a corner surrounded by bookshelves, still wearing the aviators. He was nowhere to be found. I eased into a seat by the front window, keeping my sunglasses on too. Flagging down a server, I ordered a double espresso and feigned answering a phone call, eyes fixed all the while on aviator lady.

He emerged from the restroom looking grumpy and not at all in the mood for a coffee shop afternoon. He was wearing the Panama hat today, but it was pushed awkwardly back on his head, goofy grandpa style. He must have needed a new belt or something, because his dad jeans drooped far below his waist. And his fly was open.

I sat in amazement as he grabbed, yes grabbed, the arm of a server and barked an order, jowls swinging as he spoke. She wrenched her arm away and rolled her eyes, and I got the feeling he must have been a regular and a great tipper or she would have clocked him, senior status notwithstanding. He clearly saw nothing wrong with his behavior and made his way to the waiting wingback. So not cool.

As he approached his significant other, the grumpy look seemed more angry. What on earth? Trouble in paradise? Perhaps paradise was only an idealized figment of my all-too-active imagination. He plopped down as if he'd been shoveling coal all day and muttered something I couldn't make out in an unpleasant, curmudgeonly voice. Giving as good as she got, she snapped back and said something was *his own damn fault.*

This was getting juicy. And I was loving every second of it. Sure, it was great to admire people I thought were cool, but I was finding it a lot more fun to realize they were not. Just a couple of poor old slobs dealing with life, same as the rest of us. Just because they happened to have a cool license plate and sunglasses and hats, hardly made them hipsters or cultural icons.

The argument had revved up and was now in full force. But somehow I got the feeling it wasn't an argument at all. More like a lifestyle. She took off the sunglasses, and for the first time I saw the small beady eyes, deeply set in her crinkled face, flashing with rage and disgust. It was almost as if she didn't even *like* him. From the thin, gray pony tail to the crepey skin and downturned, sunken mouth, her entire being exuded *tired*. Of him. He, on the other hand, was just tired of everything. Gone was the carefree, content demeanor of their afternoon cruises through Albuquerque.

I wasn't sure what to feel. Pity? Glee? There was certainly disappointment, but I was quickly getting beyond that and settling back into reality. And then it happened. The old curmudgeon dropped an F-bomb.

I still couldn't hear them well enough for any context. They could have been talking about politics, an overcooked breakfast, or incontinence. All I knew was that they were both by now cussing up a storm and glaring at each other, he in his mean sarcasm, she in disdain.

Others were taking notice around the coffee shop. Two young women were clearly annoyed as they tried to study in peace. An older gentleman, also donning aviators but with an impressive gray Cornel West 'fro, was reading in a corner adjacent to mine and making no effort to hide his amusement.

She was done with him. Loudly enough to be heard by just about everyone, she snarled, *Okay, fine. Let's just go.* She didn't wait but grabbed the keys and her coffee and headed for the door, shoving the sunglasses back onto her old, tired face. He had no choice but to follow. She had the keys. Skulking out behind her, fly still open, he was oblivious to his audience.

Back in the 1990s, tennis pro Andre Agassi was known for a phrase he uttered in a television commercial: *Image is everything.* In that ad, Agassi's image was supercool, white Lamborghini, dark sunglasses and all. But, as an ardent tennis fan, my focus was on the reality of his game. Although a great player, he never seemed particularly cool on the court to me. Of course, in observing celebrities there is the advantage of having more than the occasional superficial glimpse.

I still see the old couple around town now and then. Interestingly, I don't even think they're trying to portray cool. The idea of image probably doesn't enter their orbit. They're just being themselves, doing their thing, and apparently unconcerned about what anybody thinks. Now, how cool is *that*.

* * *

When in Doubt (A Rant)

I've heard more than a few negative comments about my refusal to partake in social media. *That's pretty strange in this day and age. How can you even conduct day to day life without it? Don't you want to stay engaged, to know what people are saying and doing?* No.

Here's the gist. I am a very private person. There are very few select people in this world whose counsel and opinion I trust and respect. I do not care what anyone else is saying or doing, or whether anyone else "likes" what I'm saying or doing.

The advent of the Internet, or more particularly social media, is largely responsible for this steadfast stance of mine. This is because of two glaring (and terrifying) results of the phenomenon.

23

First, we are no longer a society of thinkers. We don't have to be. Why should we invest the energy it takes to drum up thoughts of our own, when we can just sit back and have them fed to us? I liken it to a baby who is completely dependent on parents and sitters for their nutritional sustenance. The baby doesn't have to make informed choices about the wisdom or health benefits of a meal and its ingredients. Only, we're not babies.

There's a saying I've quoted for as long as I can remember: *When in doubt, THINK!* I've long attributed it to my mom, who was full of wise sayings, but in truth it may have just been one of my typical sardonic retorts to some nonsense or other and has now become a mantra. In any event, it seems more apropos today than ever. Thinking has become a lost art, and apparently a monumental waste of time. Instead of thinking through a matter and reaching one's own considered conclusion, just see what the rest of the world has to say about it.

Another spawn of social media is endemic laziness. Why read? Why study actual history when one can just choose to embrace whatever alternative facts come across his or her Twitter feed? Why do the research to find out if a social media post is true or just invented for convenience's sake? Who can be so bothered? (This is largely the reason I left a career in print journalism shortly after the Internet came along. I saw the writing on the wall, although I could never have predicted the full, tragic absurdity of it all.)

There is a Scripture that tells us to "test the spirits," i.e., don't just accept/believe anything and everything that comes down the pike, but do the research and find out for yourself what's true. It's a concept that I can only hope will one day catch fire again.

Until that time comes, I'll just choose to abstain, thank you. So, for the estimated billions of social media users worldwide, great. Fine. Own your choices. And I'll own mine.

* * *

Control

From its invention, the wheel has been the purveyor of a single authority that everyone seems to crave: control.

Think of it. The change that comes over young people when they finally get their wheels, or the aggressive driver who thinks he owns the road, all because he's on four wheels. Even pushing a cart in the supermarket affords us more credence than carrying a mere handbasket, making the bold statement that we're there to do some serious shopping, for heavy stuff and not just snacks, maybe even buying in bulk!

I saw a guy on a unicycle, maneuvering expertly along a local jogging path, paying no mind to the joggers, walkers, or even bikes that were forced to go around or wait until he passed. No, his was the only game in town, and the path belonged to him.

I'm convinced that the confidence that comes with wheels is largely attributable to the quick escape they afford. We don't have to hang around for the retribution that is due any narcissistic misdeeds. Think of the police chases that are captured by news helicopters or other cameras. Where do these criminals get the hubris to think they can actually get away? *The wheels!!* They actually believe they're in control of the situation (all the while overlooking the fact that everyone else on the road, including the law enforcement officer chasing them, has wheels of their own).

On foot, that same bold driver may be the most docile person you'll ever meet, perhaps even hanging his/her head, shifting uncomfortably, unable to make eye contact. But wheels give us control, confidence, exhilaration, speed.

Then there are the conductors of wheels who are not so docile. These are the folks who may not only be concerned with the quick escape, but the actual damage wheels can do. For their purposes, wheels may be weaponized. Think of monster truck rallies. Not only is it thrilling to sit ten feet higher from the ground than everyone else, but you get to run over stuff. *Crush* things. Oh, the power, the intimidation! Surely you must be the best and the baddest.

Even in my meek, non-threatening world, I remember coming to terms with the perceived loss of superiority on the road when I traded my larger SUV for a smaller, lower one. It kind of shocked me, as I wasn't even aware I'd harbored such notions.

In some cities, street racing is a common problem. It's reckless and dangerous to the community, and a serious criminal offense even if no one is hurt or killed. But that doesn't stop the racers. Behind the wheel of a muscle car flying competitively through town, there is power. There is control (hopefully). And it's worth noting that the racers are not necessarily thugs or n'er-do-wells. Much like the overly obsessed competitors in many sports, they are often just average folks with a craving.

It may be a deep-seated, inherent need that we all have, but those who choose to exercise that imagined control through the use, or misuse, of their wheels, do so at their own peril. Once again, it would do us all well to realize that we're not the only one with wheels. And, even if we were, there are a couple of facts we must face. First, there will always be someone whose wheels are faster than our own. Secondly, *we'll eventually have to get out of the car.*

My suggestion? Find another avenue. If you must have power over others, perhaps consider brain power. Few things are more gratifying than knowing stuff that others do not. And oh, the intimidation! Moreover, there's no risk of arrest, retaliation, or crashing into a lamppost. Just think of it. Please.

* * *

Real or Not Real?

I guess I was one of the slow ones. I just didn't see it coming. Truth is, I was living overseas in a remote village in Angola with no electricity when the reality TV craze came about. I couldn't have known.

Upon returning to the States, I found the likes of *Survivor* and *Hoarders* and *Fear Factor* wholly ridiculous. But then I remembered there had long been *Divorce Court* and *The Dating Game* and *Newlywed Game.* On the humorous side, there was *America's Funniest Home Videos,* which not only provided comic relief, but also made wannabe videographers of millions.

But now we'd graduated to new genres and levels of inanity.

The whole obsession with other peoples' lives and neuroses, as phony and contrived as they are on reality TV, likely began with the advent of moving pictures and television. There, everybody's life was more interesting than our own. We knew it wasn't real, but we liked to put ourselves in others' shoes and love-lives and economic status. A little fantasy, a little escape, never hurt anyone.

Then came the hard-hitting stuff, the true on-screen reality—the news. And violence. The R-rated sex scenes on the small screen hadn't yet passed the censors' muster, but the nightly news offered up all manner of war and murder and blood and gore.

JFK and his murderer. Black and white images of dead and dying soldiers. The dogs, the hoses, the trees of strange fruit. Jackson and the others standing over a lifeless King, pointing toward that window. The blank, dying stare of RFK on the hotel kitchen floor.

Following in short order, of course, were smartphones, and with them, at long last, the ability to capture police brutality for all the world to see (and everyone finally knew Rodney King was only the tip of the iceberg).

And then there was R. Budd Dwyer. The Pennsylvania politician's horrific public suicide preceded smartphones, but his choice to commit the act during a televised press conference made up for that. The footage is still around, with a YouTube cult following that will probably never end. There were the collective gasps from reporters, friends and co-workers in the room as he drew the handgun from a manila envelope; the weapon swiftly shoved into his mouth and fired before he could be stopped; the camera closeup as blood poured like a faucet from his mouth and nostrils, the gaping hole clearly visible in the top of his head (he'd chosen a .357 Magnum to do the deed).

Sure, there was initial widespread horror. But the ensuing fascination, and near glee, of the breathless nationwide press coverage was no doubt another contributor to the spectacle we know today as reality TV.

When did the numbness, indifference, and soullessness begin?

The lust for violence and bloodshed abated somewhat, the worst of it relegated to R-rated movies and video games. Viewing audiences settled decidedly on a sex theme, always implicit and increasingly explicit, as intentional reality TV evolved. We all got together with the FCC, made necessary compromises, and settled comfortably (or uncomfortably for some of us) into the reality that is today.

In an inevitable discussion of reality TV and politics, journalist David Brooks wrote in an August 2020 New York Times op-ed:

> *Trump family values are mean world values. Mean world syndrome was a concept conceived in the 1970s by the communications professor George Gerbner. His idea was that people who see relentless violence on television begin to perceive the world as being more dangerous than it really is.*
>
> *By the 1990s it was no longer violent programming that drove mean world culture, but reality television. That's an entire industry designed to give the impression that human beings are inherently manipulative, selfish and petty. If you grow up watching these programs, or starring in them, naturally you believe that other people are fundamentally untrustworthy.*

While much of today's reality TV seems to target young people, one can't help but notice it's the topic of an awful lot of water cooler conversations among the not-so-young. As a major component of the pervasive pop culture discussed earlier, it has taken on a note of seriousness that it just doesn't warrant. And its purveyors—producers, actors, etc.—are laughing all the way to the bank.

Granted, some reality TV is so ridiculous that it's hilarious and still makes for a fun escape. But, we would do well to draw a line somewhere. At very least, we can acknowledge that even its name is a lie—because *it's not real!* What is real is the fear that intelligent adults actually believe these are real people's real lives and problems, and the viewing audience is needed to help resolve them. Yes, there are folks who actually feel a sense of urgency to call in, log on, weigh in, follow, download the app, and share their views on the comings and goings of total strangers—and actors at that. Ugghh.

Of course, there is also the obsession not just with reality TV actors' fake lives, but with celebrities' actual lives. This should be a passing interest at best, but it tends to occupy an inordinate amount of time and space in the minds of fans.

I enjoy a good novel or a psychological thriller at the movies as much as the next guy. Once again, entertainment and escape are important parts of a healthy, well-rounded lifestyle. But we always knew it was just an escape and it wasn't real. We might tell someone about it at the water cooler the next day, but what we were sharing was the imagination and creativity behind the story, not gossip about people's actual lives.

I once heard a parent tell her daughter that not everyone can be a Kardashian. I wondered if the real question should be, does everyone *want* to be a Kardashian?!

And so, here we are, and will probably remain. During those awful days of murder and mayhem, and even televised suicide, we used to say you couldn't make this stuff up. I guess it turns out you could.

* * *

Who Cares?

There's a disturbing trend afoot in the U.S.A. No, not a health care crisis, the real estate market, unemployment, immigration or the economy. History has shown that these all come and go, and probably always will.

No, our current dilemma is of our own making, and although bells and whistles are screaming warnings at record decibels, many of us refuse to even recognize there's trouble up ahead.

Do you remember the old John Candy/Steve Martin movie, *Planes, Trains and Automobiles*? There's a scene in which the two crazy cohorts are driving at night along a highway but in the wrong direction, with oncoming traffic just ahead. A car pulls alongside them facing the opposite direction and the driver yells a warning, "You're going the wrong way!" Undeterred, the two just laugh it off, asking one another, "How does HE know where we're going?"

We all may as well be passengers in that car. We're going the wrong way, and we're ignoring all warnings. One must wonder what might be the consequence of such willful ignorance over the long term.

The age-old disease of apathy has spread through our population like California wildfires, leaving in its wake a path of destruction that may now be irreparable.

There was a time when we were faulted as a society full of greedy workaholics, our "eyes on the prize" in a dog-eat-dog, Machiavellian pursuit in which we repeatedly reassured ourselves that the end would justify the means to whatever lofty goals we'd set.

Now, that wasn't the ideal image, mind you. But, at least we *had* goals. Back in the eighties, we yuppies may have been working ourselves to death to amass wealth that we could not take with us, but at least we believed we had a reason for what we were doing. Today, more of us seem to be spinning our wheels without a clue, or a care, as to why we're doing it.

Sadly, there are those ninety-nine percenters who are so deflated by the knee of the one percent on their necks that they've given up aspirations of achieving anything. Again, at least there is a basis for such thinking.

How many of us live in certain neighborhoods, adhere to particular diets, drive particular cars, join clubs or churches, and even practice certain hobbies, without any real reason, or only because someone else does?

Think of some of the mindless blather on television. Or, even worse, the households in which the television is on 24/7 with no one even listening to the mindless blather. Those televisions are on for the same reason that people climb mountains.

When we reach the point of doing things for no reason, not even a defeatist, pathetic or imbecilic one, we're in trouble.

I'm reminded of the folks who insist on having the latest model luxury automobile or smartphone (because it's there), but fail to notice that their bodies have deteriorated to an advanced state of decrepitude for lack of proper upkeep. Now, farbeit from me to tell anyone how to spend their money, but…

Then there are those who spring for the full 600-channel cable package every month and have no idea what is the content of 550 of those channels.

While on the journey down this slippery slope, one glimmer of hope emerged during the year of the pandemic. Folks stepped up. Got creative. Engaged. Even cared.

As we inch our way back to normal, perhaps it's a good time to open our eyes. Maybe there are changes to be made, maybe not, but at least let's be aware of what we're doing and not keep going full speed ahead blindly, mindlessly.

Apathy is a disease, a contagious one, that is fast becoming a plague in our society. We're going the wrong way. Does anybody care?

* * *

The Hatred Within

If someone says, "I love God," and hates his brother, he is a liar; for he who does not love his brother whom he has seen, how can he love God whom he has not seen? 1 John 4:20

Jesus said to him, " 'You shall love the LORD your God with all your heart, with all your soul, and with all your mind.' ³⁸ This is the first and great commandment. ³⁹ And the second is like it: 'You shall love your neighbor as yourself.' ⁴⁰ On these two commandments hang all the Law and the Prophets." Matthew 22:36-40

To whom do these tenets apply? To whom do the Commandments apply? Who is your brother? Who is your neighbor?

According to a 2015 Gallup poll, 75% of Americans professed Christianity, but only 24% believe the Bible is the literal word of God, and 47% believe it is the "inspired" word of God. That explains a lot. If everyone believed it was God's word, they might be expected to obey it. All of it. Selectivity is much more convenient—freedom to quote, preach, and judge when one feels it is warranted, but without obligation to adhere to what's just not comfortable.

So, I can love whomever I want. And I can hate, abuse and oppress anyone I don't care for…anyone who's not like me, or doesn't agree with me, or threatens my sense of superiority. Really?

We're a funny country. If we're being honest, we largely believe we're better than other countries. And much of that nationalism stems from the notion that we're a "Christian" country, at least according to many evangelicals. (Of course, one would be hard-pressed to explain how it is that a pluralistic country can profess a singular religion.) But, following that train of thought, if Christianity is what makes us better or superior, and we fail to behave as Christians, then are we….worse? Inferior?

The growing hatred among us, its ever more violent and terrifying manifestations, and the license to perpetuate it that has come from the very top, MUST give us pause. Christian or not, there simply MUST be a time of reckoning, a "come to Jesus" moment, if you will.

Here are a few ideas to kick around:

You're not better than anyone. You have no right to abuse or oppress anyone. And no one American life matters any less than another. Period. If you choose to hate, then go ahead and hate. That's between you and your maker. But you have no right to manifest that hate by your actions, and certainly not in the name of a God who loves all.

Mutual respect and dignity are Christian tenets, like it or not and, if you call yourself a Christian, you don't get to choose if or when to abide by them. And if you're not a Christian, perhaps just consider the legal and moral obligations that come with being human.

Either way, the upshot is clear. Keep your hate to yourself.

* * *

Chilling

Is it just me, or has anxiety become our middle name? It's everywhere. There's even a disorder named after it.

Like many things, anxiety has also become trendy. (Hear me out on this.) When it comes to our mental health, we're talking about serious issues—chemical imbalance, PTSD, and the like are worthy foes that many people fight valiantly for years, or even a lifetime. But some very serious conditions are also used as fallbacks, convenient excuses, or simply attention-grabbers. One can almost pinpoint the moment when suddenly *everybody* had OCD, or a gluten allergy, or a clown phobia. They were the latest hipster disorders. (An emotional support peacock? Really, people?)

Of course, the saddest and cruelest aspect of falsely and flippantly claiming any illness for self-serving purposes is that the true sufferers are robbed of credibility and even access to treatment.

Also lamentable are those who really believe they're afflicted with something when they are not. The power of suggestion is, well, powerful. We can be so easily convinced that something's wrong with us. A quick perusal of just about any page on WebMD, and you'll know you are surely dying. And personal injury lawyers' commercials are the greatest pain and sickness inducers ever created.

I remember a hilarious episode of *Frazier* that had Niles convinced he was high after thinking he'd consumed a pot brownie. He hadn't, but his response to the suggestion was like a hippie right out of the 70s.

Then there are the cures for all the "anxiety" out there. The prospect of taking real meds for fake diseases should scare us all back to reality. Lots of folks who may not have anxiety disorder but just guess or assume they probably do, are also turning to CBD, and many swear by its calming effects. Having yet to be scientifically proven, it's entirely possible that CBD does indeed help some people who really need help. But, having seen trends and fads come and go over a lifetime, I have to wonder just how many people are being helped. Could it be that some folks are, like Niles, reacting the way they think they're supposed to react to perceived treatments for perceived afflictions?

The confusion over real and imagined anxiety disorders became especially troubling with the onset of COVID-19 and all that came with it. A novel virus, with full effects yet unknown and vaccine distribution even today still being sorted out, most certainly gave rise to circumstantial anxiety around the world. Whether everyone was suddenly suffering from a disorder was another story.

Possibly the one good outcome of this temporary, virus-related condition was the serious, rather than flippant, pursuit of self-care. There was a noticeable shift in attitudes. Many people understood pretty quickly that we were in uncharted waters. It was now clear that anxiety was a real thing, and that due to quarantine they would need to combat it on their own, at least to some extent. They resorted to prayer and meditation, exercise, improved eating habits (as a bonus, home cooking equaled less spending), drinking less (or more), and concerted efforts to improve relationships. Some of these were endeavors that had been neglected for years.

In the forced slowing down that came with Covid, we were also better able to embrace and appreciate the self-care that had always been available to us, much of which came with valuing relationships. Some people even discovered that solitude could actually be a good thing. (See? Told you.)

In the process of learning to chill, some folks realized they had no disorder at all. Finally understanding that, yes, bad stuff happens, and yes, sometimes even to them, they grew up, surrendered their privilege and entitlement, stopped worrying about the newest trend in afflictions, and got serious about taking care of their own health and household.

Of course, there were many who would have none of such real-world notions. But, let's give kudos to those who chose introspection and actual self-improvement.

And all it took was a global pandemic.

* * *

People and Their Nonsense

He was a small man, less than 5'8", having inherited his slight stature from his father. Only in his dad's day and in his dad's culture, it wasn't such a big deal. Today in America it was. Fortunately he felt no need to compensate. In fact, he was amused at those who did. Comfortable in his own skin, neither an obsessed bodybuilder or a loudmouth, he loved pro tennis and Yo Yo Ma and a good Cab. And his work.

He'd written for five different publications in an eventful 40-year career, including a stint with the AP while based in Hong Kong. As in so many of life's endeavors, the best part was the people. Twice offered an editorship, he'd preferred to stay on the beat because of the people. Age, gender, ethnicity, career, socioeconomic standing, it mattered not. Getting a scoop was always exciting, especially if it involved politics or scandal. But the true fascination was the people. Everyone had a story, and the man loved communicating their stories to his readers, weaving the mundane, the unlikely, and even the criminal accounts into vivid narratives. This year, for the first time, he'd begun to wonder if the people and their stories had changed, or if he had.

Proudly apolitical, he was a registered Independent. As had always been mandatory from his old-school journalism studies, any personal political beliefs were a nonentity in his work life. These days, the people seemed at odds with this longstanding wont. (Even some of his fellow journalists were now interspersing their own opinion into their work.) And the people were becoming more aggressive. Where it once was like pulling teeth to get a direct answer, now they just wouldn't shut up, rambling on incessantly about their own preferred topic rather than the interview questions posed to them. In the year 2020, that topic was politics.

If he asked a question about Covid, the answer was political. About education, health care, the economy, still political.

He had always been a straight shooter, not easily rattled, patient enough to develop a rapport with his subjects but having little tolerance for nonsense. This year, he felt that comfortable groove approaching its end. He knew that end may finally have arrived when he was told by an interviewee that as an Asian he should love Trump. (And this in answer to a query about how a potential new administration might affect the local economy.)

The man had met his future wife in college in his early 20s. Almost immediately they'd discovered important common ground in their respective belief systems: if some jerk had a problem with them, it was the jerk's problem, not theirs. Both his Korean and Chinese families and her Somali American family had drilled it into them from their youth—never apologize for who you are. Over the years, she'd had opportunity to instill the creed into some of her university students, sometimes offering off-campus counsel to those struggling for acceptance in their new Ivy League atmosphere.

The couple had always been each other's rock, frequently reminding one another that some things would never change. Narrow minds would not miraculously expand, no more than pandemics would miraculously disappear. But they had at least hoped for gradual progress. Today, they looked up and realized it had been forty years—maybe a little too gradual.

That "helpful" voting advice he'd received was turning hostile. It came to a head when he discovered that apparently he personally had brought coronavirus to America, the shocking truth being revealed by yet another interviewee who was supposed to be talking about the local food bank.

When he called his wife to share this new information, the news that he himself had been the conveyor of the virus, she sensed he had reached a boiling point and she would have to talk him down lest he finally open his mouth and allow all manner of career-ending rage to pour forth. (They'd often made bets as to whose career would be the first to reach this inauspicious conclusion.)

They were talking more about retirement of late. The grand plan had always been to do all they could to stay healthy and then ride off into the sunset at around seventy. They were just a few years short of that, but the current cultural and political environment was clearly indicating a change of plans was in order.

It was the people and their nonsense. Those he'd once loved interviewing but now feared he was beginning to hold in disdain.

His wife reminded him once again that there was nothing new under the sun. People's views hadn't changed. Folks felt the same way they always had, displaying the same ignorant behavior the couple had seen in the early days of their marriage. No, the people and their views were still there. Only now they'd been encouraged out of the woodwork and given a license to let their hate flag fly.

She was right, of course.

The man was covering a City Council meeting that evening, with an agenda that included church pastors airing grievances about mandatory mask wearing, the School Board discussing virtual learning and a budget to get laptops to the kids who needed them, etc., etc., etc.

He knew a little self-care might be needed before he took off. A brandy and a little Yo Yo Ma would do the trick. Closing his eyes for a moment, he marveled yet again at how the master's cello could capture the heartache and poverty of Appalachia.

He cried.

* * *

The Odyssey of Art

Please Go Home and
Burn Your Shoes

I just signed up for the annual tango festival. It's an exhilarating gathering of dancers and instructors from all over the world, one of several annual events that has put our fair city on the map. But, unlike Balloon Fiesta, this is a unique community, and not of ballroom dancers, but aficionados of the very distinct, breathtakingly beautiful Argentine tango descending upon Albuquerque every fall.

I've attended for several years now. I have no idea why I keep going. I will never be satisfied with my mastery of this craft, but few people are. Periodically I vow to stop doing this to myself and never return.

I have a number of acquaintances who are multi-lingual, and I myself get by pretty well in a couple of languages besides English. But, for me it doesn't come easily. Unlike some, I cannot switch effortlessly from one language to another, or fluidly navigate a conversation in a language not my first. It doesn't come naturally. It is not a gift. I must think about it, work at it.

Such is the case with tango. I'm amazed at those for whom it does seem to flow so naturally, as if they were born on the dance floor. I'm enthralled at their beauty. I'm just not one of them. The mechanics are there, but they don't necessarily flow. Yes, I do get lost in the dance, but not always in a good way. Even after years of practice (albeit not without long breaks to sulk in frustration), it just doesn't come easily.

And yet, I persist.

I once watched an interview with a 28-year-old professional tennis player. While his career had yielded some success, even glimmers of greatness, he was still relatively unknown and perpetually broke. He'd just failed to qualify for the U.S. Open.

When asked if he was considering broadcasting or some other tennis-related profession that might actually pay the bills, he shot an incredulous look at the interviewer and answered an emphatic *No.*

It was simply inconceivable that this dedicated young player would even consider doing anything else but play tennis. Period.

Yes, it's torturous, a form of masochism. But, there are some things that we Simply. Must. Do. There is no choice. We don't have to be great at these things, or earn a living or a following or any accolades. Something in us just dictates that we persist.

Painters, musicians, writers all know what this is. Unlike a drug or alcohol addiction, it is something else, something that is intrinsic to our very being. There is not a question of whether we'll indulge this compulsion. We must. We can't not. (And we don't regret it later when we fall down, either literally or figuratively.)

And so, I will not go home and burn my shoes, as tempted as I may be at times. I will not stop taking lessons or save the hundreds of dollars I invest in the annual festival. I'll show up, endure the highs and lows, the great leads and the horrid ones. I'll shrug off the judgment and condescension of the hoity toity dancers. I'll bask in the music and the beauty of the masters' performances. And I'll tell myself, once again, that next year will be even better.

* * *

Michelangelo and Me

On a recent re-reading of *The Agony and the Ecstasy*, I was reminded yet again that there are few figures in history more captivating, and more painfully beautiful, than Michelangelo Buonarroti. A quote from the hypnotic volume stays with me always: *He simply had no talent for social amenities, nor any liking for society. He was as solitary as though he were dead. The tighter he bolted his studio door against the intrusion of the outside world, the more evident it became that trouble was man's natural state.*

Often the life of a loner or an introvert is borne not of any particular contempt for the outside world (although that may be part of it), but simply that we don't *get* the outside world. Some of us may examine society around us for a time before arriving at the informed conclusion that we have no desire to be a part of it; others just know inherently, without ever having been fully immersed. I think Michelangelo was of the latter ilk. I get it. I get him.

For some, there is simply no ability, nor any desire, to verbally communicate innermost thoughts or passions, or to understand those of others. This, too, can often come after a period of trial and error. After all, we're taught from a young age to be social beings. But, even as early as elementary school, we may notice that whenever we open our mouths, try to participate or interact, we somehow just don't fit. Those who try eventually resign themselves to the truth that no one else exists in their orbit.

Rather than solipsism, this is just a natural state of solitude. Often, if there was a way to fit in, they would. But they have no problem accepting their reality.

As this group is often comprised of artists, they can then indulge in the comically absurd art of self-entertainment. And, when they stumble across someone else who gets it, albeit six hundred years later, they fall head over heels. For, this natural state was not unique to the Renaissance era, or even to the artists of the time, but it is perpetual.

Michelangelo's passion for his gift and calling, his lifestyle, loves and the deepest desires of his soul, could not be expressed in words, but only through his work. He spoke volumes while rarely uttering a word. He possessed, as so many artists do, the unique ability to amuse himself, to produce his work and not obsess over whether the entire world loved it.

Such unusual qualities are the foundation of the love many of us today still have for him. We exist on the same plane and identify with him on an extraordinary level (except for that whole genius thing, of course).

Those lifelong love affairs that are so rare any more, the 70-year marriages and friendships, transcend words. This was true of an interview I watched during the pandemic summer, when a woman whose friend of fifty years was lost to the virus found herself unable to complete the interview. There simply were no words.

Mutual trust, respect and admiration must certainly be components of such relationships—elements that may be taken lightly these days, but in truth are so profound that they can be communicated through art rather than words.

Only this can explain the profound friendship between a simple, 21st-century lover of literature and a 16th-century Renaissance artist who still possesses the undying admiration of millions. And this notwithstanding the fact that he was 5'4" and crazy as a loon. No matter. Our lifelong friendship continues, and I look forward to the long, deep conversations we'll have when I get to heaven. I know he's there, year by year welcoming those of us who get him.

* * *

The Books

My books, my precious books. What will become of them? It was a foreboding that gripped me and would not let go.

A good friend once told me about the ancient Hebrew custom of ethical wills. They are a way to leave with loved ones a true understanding of what really matters, the ethical values that transcend monetary bequests, etc.

As I embarked on the journey of composing an ethical will, which I decided to call a legacy letter, I considered the priorities, the things that mattered most and how best to communicate their import. A sense of sadness soon overcame me. It was a truth that I preferred to avoid—no matter how important an object or a cause or a viewpoint might be to me, some things were not likely to matter to anyone else. My beloved library was one of those things.

There were Aristotle, Homer and More (formerly owned by my mother); Shakespeare, Dostoyevsky and Hugo, Hemingway and Bronte(s), Giovanni, St. Vincent Millay and Poe; Angelou and Baldwin and Ellison, Wiesel and Achebe, du Bois, Morrison, Meacham, Kearns-Goodwin, Chernow and Obama; there were Grisham and Turow…and I licked my lips and took a deep breath and dried my eyes as I considered my great love for Gabriel Garcia Marquez. There were the tango books, and the books on writing, and anthropology, and American government, and Bonhoeffer, Lewis and St. Augustine. There were the Bibles in a dozen different languages.

Who would care? They would most likely all be relegated to some musty attic or basement, or donated to something or someone who would in turn relegate them there. But not read. Not caressed, or even handled. Not employed as a reference for that classic, delicious phrase that had slipped someone's mind, or meditated upon or quoted when discussing the issues that matter.

Why do you keep them, someone once asked. *You can get everything digitally now.* Well, of course I know that. I don't *want* everything digitally. I love my books, and I want my descendants to love them too.

I love Kalamata olives. I know few others, at least in my immediate circle, who do. It is simply not possible to *make* someone want something or develop a taste for something, and in most cases I got that. So why was it so important to me now?

Even though I consider great literature to be tantamount to a great meal, it is not only the ingredients I want others to savor. It is the medium.

In so many aspects of 21st-century life, much is missing. In fact, there are great chasms, voids that desperately need to be filled. Soundbites and synopses and summations can be had anywhere at any time, usually in the interest of "saving" –time, effort, whatever. I would posit that nothing is being saved, but much is being lost, particularly in light of what is being done with that extra time and effort.

Okay, so yes, we have different priorities and affections. To each her own. But are we sacrificing our wholeness? Because something new is available, does it mean we no longer need the old? Granted, there are many shortcuts and conveniences for which no one is more grateful than I. But not those that will surely rob me of a portion of my soul, my substance, my depth.

I recently learned of an app that "helps" people to be calm and less anxious, by scheduling brief increments during the day of listening to relaxing music, or deep breathing, yoga, and whatever else folks apparently need an app in order to do. I find this not unlike signing up for dinner ingredients to be delivered in order for me to be able to prepare a meal. (If I ever become that incapable of controlling my own 24-hour days, please shoot me.)

I find my time of morning prayer and meditation absolutely essential to my wholeness, as are my detox baths, stretching and breathing exercises, healthy meals, etc.—and I don't even need anyone to tell me how to do these things, or to schedule them for me.

Likewise, it is critical to the nurturing of my soul to be still and read on a regular basis. Not on an electronic device that is sure to ring or buzz or pop up an interrupting message of some sort, but curled up in bed or in front of a fire or in a quiet corner of a library or even a coffee shop or airport. It is the departure from the noise of life, that aforementioned delicious meal that I look forward to, the anticipatory turning of pages, the gratification of the next scene, the next unforgettable quixotic or shocking or heartwrenching turn of a phrase.

The tragic but certain loss to my granddaughters of this fullness, this richness of soul, was a reality I could not bear. As I wondered how to articulate the importance of the books in my legacy letter, I realized I could not. I tried to remember how my mother had communicated it to me. Well, kind of by force. But, while she could force me to read, she couldn't make me savor. She had nothing to do with the addiction.

And so I abandoned the effort. Sure, I wrote about my deep love for the books and how I treasured them, as best I knew how to express it. But the hope that someone else would treasure them was lost, and I had to face this truth. Deep down, I still wanted to be wrong about this (and considering family history, I probably was). I decided not to argue about it with myself any further. My granddaughters were quite likely to embrace a love of literature all by themselves. But I still allowed myself a time of loss and mourning and reflection. Oh, the books, the books…

* * *

Tango Fixes Everything

Four o'clock. The man had spent much of the afternoon pondering the merits of robbing a Brink's truck. Not that he had any intention of doing so, or ever would dare an illegal act. But sitting in interstate traffic behind one of the impenetrable mobile boxes, the notion had struck him that it probably wouldn't be that hard to rob. Who knew why such a thing would crash into his already inexplicable thought process, and why he would spend two hours of his life exploring it? Well, didn't the likes of da Vinci spend countless hours dreaming up all sorts of random stuff? Oh, that's right, his musings were actually productive and made a contribution to civilized society. Damn.

Sometimes these mental wanderings provided a needed escape, and he freely allowed himself to go there whenever reality was just too hard. Today was one of those days.

It was an overcast New Mexico morning, and everything looked so very bleak. Everything. He was already in his late forties. When did *that* happen? Yes, from the absurdity of being unemployed for the first time in 20 years, to the rejection of his latest break-up, everything in his life seemed to loom and lurk and threaten. His adult twin daughters were doing okay with their life choices so far, but precariously so. These days he was constantly worried they would follow in their mom's footsteps and choose the self-destructive path she'd been on since the divorce eight years earlier.

Even as he made plans for the upcoming tango festival, cynicism ruled the day. He'd probably spend a grand to attend the thing and then have a lousy time. How was the perpetual sense of foreboding ever to be defeated? It held an iron grip of power over him, crushing any hope he dared fancy.

He probably shouldn't even be going, given his current financial woes, but there was never a question that he would. A few dollars could be saved if he shared the Air BNB that some of his friends were planning to rent, but there was no chance of that either. The man could barely stand living with himself, let alone someone else, even for a few days.

As he sat stock still behind the Brink's truck, a massive Winnebago to his left, it suddenly began to rain torrents. His least favorite place to be, in the worst possible conditions. He broke for a mental escape, considering what was behind his constant shift from staunch determination to attend a crowded festival, to quietly plotting to go off the grid.

For quite awhile now, he'd thought the thing out pretty thoroughly—he could well do without TV, internet and the like. His kids were grown and could come visit whenever they wanted. But for now he desperately needed to not hear people's voices for a good long while. The whining, complaining, debating, the politics, the bureaucracy. He was done. But he still wanted to dance. It had become the unfailing ray of light in a world that was gloomier by the day. Was there tango off the grid?

The Brink's truck inched forward and his mind wandered back to the festival. Maybe his leading proficiency had improved enough for some of the better follows to actually accept his cabeceo.

Maybe his years of lessons wouldn't abandon him. Who knows, if he closed his eyes right then and there, turned on Piazzolla and focused real hard, the sun would probably come out. Yes, surely all would be well. Because, when all is said and done, tango fixes everything.

* * *

Beauty

Roger Federer's one-handed backhand. Pavarotti's Nessun Dorma. My granddaughters. Ennio Morricone's Gabriel's Oboe. Frida Kahlo's self-portraits. Misty Copeland's Giselle. Victor Hugo's Les Miserables. Michelangelo's David. Ellena Chavez dancing the tango. Yo Yo Ma's Appalachian Waltz. Gabriel Garcia Marquez' One Hundred Years of Solitude. Alfie Boe's Jean Valjean. Jake Shimabukura's Ave Maria. New Mexico sunsets.

Marvel, embrace, indulge, escape, but take none of it for granted. Be it your own personal beauty or art that only you know, and no one else could appreciate, or the unfathomable God-given gifts possessed by others but available for us all to enjoy freely, lavish in it. Because the heartbreaking truth is, not everyone can.

Think of those who will never see a sunset, or their grandchildren's faces, or will never visit a museum, or see or hear the works of the masters. Or those who once did experience such beauty but never will again, and what they would give to have just a moment more.

Subjective, yes. There's that whole "eye of the beholder" thing. No matter. Simply consider what is beauty to *you,* and run with it. It is what feeds your individual soul, whether you know it or not. It is your sustenance.

* * *

The Gift

There is a particular artistry to great diction. Not necessarily perfect diction, mind you, but great nonetheless.

Beauty can be found in idioms unique to particular cultures or regions of a country. Enunciation can be mesmerizing. The turn of a phrase, or even a singular word applied unexpectedly can yield great delight when properly appreciated. Stop and contemplate, as one would in a museum and, oh my!

Diction that is representative of a region is enjoyable just in the recognition of it, i.e., the way DeNiro embodies New York. Then there is the manner of speech that is simply delicious. Delectable. Gorgeous.

When the late Texas Congresswoman Barbara Jordan spoke, I stopped. It didn't matter what I was doing. I was captivated by the sound of her voice and her impeccable, beautiful diction. Sure, she was discussing the weighty matters of lawmaking, but to this hearer nothing was more important than mentally unwrapping the precious gift of her words, slowly, deliberately savoring each one.

Some of my favorite literature contains words and phrases and entire paragraphs that are so artistically transcendent that I have to read them aloud. What a grave disservice it would be if I didn't take the greatest care in doing so. The words are like a great meal, or a great wine. How sad that in our hurry-up culture we fail to take the time to appreciate each flavor and note and nuance—to give the words their due.

In a discussion or a debate or even an argument, there is a certain urgency to make one's point, to be heard and to be understood. Many people resort to yelling or cursing or name calling to accomplish this goal. Wouldn't it be more effective to simply enunciate well? Wouldn't it better capture the attention of the listener?

There is also a certain expedience to great diction. With slang, the hearer must be culturally aware in order to know what on earth the speaker is talking about. And the aforementioned yelling only turns the audience off. So, beyond appreciation for the beauty of the spoken word, it affords us one, final reward. Not only is it a tremendous timesaver, getting us neatly to the point and commanding our hearers' attention, but it saves Siri and Alexa a great deal of frustration.

* * *

Odysseus and Me: Ruminations

To Think, Perchance to Speak

I once heard the writer Malcolm Gladwell describe the differences between thinking and talking. To paraphrase, he said thinking affords us limitless liberties of time, nuance and digression. Talking, on the other hand, must be audience-focused, condensed, censored—i.e., no longer your true and complete thoughts.

When in deep thought, I get lost. Often. I wander, I dilly-dally, I shrink into a field of sunflowers, leap from a tall bridge, or meander into a maze of mystery. Complete autonomy begets reckless abandon. Or blind terror. The time, effort and energy are mine to risk or not. Curious thinkers will most always choose the risk.

How limiting it is to attempt to convey those exhilarating explorations and discoveries via the spoken the word. Be it intimate conversation or public address, it is simply and maddeningly impossible to fully think out loud (contrary to what Ed Sheeran would have us believe—for, even in song, there are limitations).

Other media do not constrain us in this way. On a recent visit to Florence, while gazing yet again upon the marvel that is David, I noticed something that rendered me dumbfounded—a vein in his right arm. How had I never seen this before?

One of my life's delights had become trekking off to Florence and contemplating David, largely because of my amazement at what Michelangelo was able to express through the medium of marble. His loves and joys, his bitterness and frustration, his soul's angst and peace, all poured through his sculpture, unlimited, unfettered.

And now, this. It was as if the maestro was speaking the words, "Oh, and one more thing…"

I often shy away from conversation beyond required dialog at work or in other business settings. I don't care for obligatory small talk, but I also avoid anything too profound. I once relished a good debate, but I just can't be so bothered any more. This is sometimes because I know the words simply don't exist to express what I'm thinking, and I know my audience won't get the fullness of it (maybe the words are there and I just haven't discovered them or can't summon them in a timely fashion); or, there's just not enough time to say it all. Like Michelangelo, I want to elaborate— perhaps adding a vein or smoothing over muscle tone. Rather than hog the conversation, I prefer to keep my mouth shut.

So, what to do?

I've known some of those gifted with an artistry like painting or sculpting, singing or playing an instrument, to suggest how very gratifying it is to be able to express themselves through their art, and I have no doubt that it is. But they are the few and the chosen.

As a writer, my initial instinct is to simply put pen to paper and write what I have to say, serving the dual purpose of expressing and memorializing my thoughts. Yes, there are still constraints, and compromises must be made (painful truths from my days as a newspaperwoman). But, for some of us, writing is still preferable to actual verbal conversation. With other people, no less.

In writing, we get to ramble incessantly, even nonsensically if we so choose, so long as we don't care if no one reads what we've written. Expressing oneself to another person and wanting or needing someone to understand, is another story.

I suppose another option is to seek to increase my vocabulary, my recall of concise words and expressions, and practice the art of succinctness in order to say all that I want in a palatable format and timetable. This would be my suggestion for those who do relish oral communication.

But for me? Naaah.

Alas, my considered, chosen mode of expression is thinking. Granted, through this medium I can only express myself to myself, but I am a captive, delighted and ever-present audience. If anyone cares to know what I think, let the spirited wordplay begin! I think.

(If, upon publication hereof, Orwell's Thought Police have become a reality, please disregard all of the above.)

* * *

Profundity

It was a day for reflection, a day for deepest thoughts, a time to ponder the impossible mysteries of life. For hours I'd wondered in awe at the moon, the stars, love and hate, joy and melancholy.

Now it was late afternoon and I sat sipping tea, reading my mail, half-watching television but still immersed in thought, now grappling with the age-old question: *Why can't white people dance?*

Inconsequential, yes, but still a valid question.

Suddenly an old video appeared on the screen, Justin Timberlake on his quest to bring sexy back. I quickly determined that my question did not hold sufficient merit for me to invest more time in it. On to other matters…

* * *

The Lockout: A Travel Odyssey

There could be little doubt that something was afoot. Something just didn't *feel* right. Was my typical business stride a little off balance? The perfect positioning of notebook, pen, business card holder in my purse?

No, it was a sound. Or lack of one. The noisy jingling of the heavy, trinket-laden keyring was not to be heard upon every movement of my purse as was usually the case. I observed the absence and then ignored it (as I am wont to do). It had been a long week of business travel and my flight home was about to touch down. The gnawing, back-of-my-mind awareness just wasn't enough to hold my attention. Yet.

Hurrying through the terminal at my usual brisk pace, I made my way to the waiting shuttle that would take me to my car. On board the shuttle, I even managed to neglect my typical routine of taking out a tip for the driver, my parking lot ticket…and my keys. Subconsciously, I must have known.

Truth could no longer be avoided, as it was now all but slapping me in the face. The driver had carried my bag to the car and stood there awkwardly for just a moment before skulking off, clearly annoyed that his tip didn't seem to be my first priority—in fact, the panicked look on my face probably said I wasn't even thinking about a tip.

Standing there alone, I felt blindly around my oversized purse, then more intently, then frantically. It was late. I was tired and wanted to go home. Was this really happening? Peering through the car windows, I tried to see if the keys were lying on the seat or the floor, but I could see nothing. Surely they were in there. Thankful that my phone still had battery life, I dialed AAA.

After praying, deep breathing, watching the gorgeous New Mexico sun set outside the covered parking structure, and being eyed suspiciously by fellow travelers and shuttle drivers, I breathed a sigh of relief when the truck pulled in an hour later. The driver, looking as tired and miserable as

I felt, ambled over and got right to work. Within minutes the door was open and, under the beam of his flashlight, I was searching the car for the keys that I knew were there. They were not. Okay. What to do?

I'm a fearless traveler. As I've gotten older, I've come to understand that there's no time for fear on Planet Carla. (I do, however, generously allow for annoyance, eye rolling and disgusted sighing.) My pragmatic bent quickly leads me to just figure it out and get on with it. And so I did.

The AAA driver said he could hotwire it for me, but that would cause the alarm to go off (continuously), and I also wouldn't be able to turn the car off. Bad plan.

Now, mind you, I had spare keys at home, but I was also locked out of the house. I called my apartment management company's emergency number, certain that I could at least get into my house that night. I was told I'd called the right number and they would be happy to unlock my door. In the morning.

Of course, my only two close friends both happened to be out of town. Of course. Still thankful for my phone, I found a hotel reservation, called an Uber and got on with it. After checking in, and by now exhausted and hungry, I made my way to the hotel bar to grab a bite to take to my room. An assortment of drunk ne'er-do-wells immediately attempted to pick me up, clearly having no understanding of how close they were to being punched out by a woman on the edge.

Surely everyone experiences those days, those comedy-of-errors events in life. For some, they seem not to be the exception, but the norm. I've long since learned to laugh them off. What else?

The next morning brought sunny skies, early entry into my apartment and retrieval of my car from the airport. Another day on Planet Carla.

* * *

Winning the Battle

War is a funny thing. Not "ha ha" funny, but peculiar. Wars are always there, happening somewhere in the world. Always. The Bible tells us that one of the signs of the end of times will be "wars and rumors of wars." I find this perplexing, because when have there *not* been wars and rumors of wars?

When it comes to war, people tend to fall into one of three camps. There are the war buffs who know every shot that was fired, by whom and on what date; the faint of heart, or nonviolence advocates, who just find even talk of war disturbing; or, those for whom war, especially in history, is one big yawn.

History is a funny thing too, due in part to revisionism. There are the assumptions and ill-conceived notions not based on fact but on theory, imagination, faulty memory, or high school lessons that amounted to little more than a large-scale telephone game.

Either way, in most cases only the true aficionados have ever bothered to consider the untold or little-known history, the idiosyncrasies and personalities inevitably associated with wars of old. Consider, for example, the hotly contested, make-or-break-our-country Civil War, and its Battle of Secessionville (also known as the Battle of James Island). Yes, there was a place called Secessionville, near Charleston, SC, and there remains a national historic district there bearing the same name. And a very important battle took place there.

The story of the Battle of Secessionville at first blush may read like every other tragic, deadly Civil War battle. And, of course, we know the end of the story. But getting to that end from Secessionville involved a few detours. First, the battle was never even supposed to be fought. But on June 16, 1862, Union Commander Henry Benham disobeyed an order forbidding any attack on Charleston and did indeed lead his forces in the Union's one and only attempt to capture Charleston by land. What compelled him? Maybe he was emboldened by the fact that his soldiers outnumbered the Confederates by three to one (each side lost about ten percent of their number). Or, maybe it was just a rare flash of rebellion in an otherwise spotless military career.

Whatever the motivation to this serious insubordination, it was to no avail. The Union suffered a devastating defeat, and Confederate Commander Thomas Lamar was hailed a hero. So yes, in some respects just another Civil War skirmish. But oh, the aftermath…

Benham was relieved of his command, arrested and court-martialed following the battle. Some accounts contend he was exonerated by the Judge Advocate General (JAG) but never given another field command. Others say the JAG wanted to convict but exoneration came through the Lincoln Administration, and Benham did indeed command other operations. No matter. He died a free man in New York at the age of 71.

More curious is the fate of the Confederacy's 24th South Carolina Infantry Regiment. Despite their new celebrity status, or maybe because of it, they were transferred to Mississippi immediately after Secessionville. Why? Was there a desperate need for newly minted heroes in Mississippi? Weren't there more battles to be fought in South Carolina?

History tells us they also fought in Tennessee, Georgia and North Carolina before ultimately surrendering with the rest of the Confederacy in 1865.

So, the proverbial winning-the battle-but-losing-the-war lesson was realized by the boys of the 24th, their short-lived heroism but a vapor. Suffice it to say those brave lads with their deep southern roots and their willingness to die for the furtherance of slavery probably didn't finish out their stay on earth in New York.

* * *

What Doesn't Kill You

Of all the ups and downs of life, the good and bad experiences, the experience of survival is a relative one. In a humorous vein, one may survive a lousy workday or a miserable date. In serious situations, a cancer survivor, for example, may prefer the term *overcomer* or *victor.*

True survival likely involves a battle of some sort. With that inevitably comes a depletion of energy and endurance. Such loss would demand there be a takeaway, a lesson, growth. There must be an assessment of what remains. How much energy, or money, or health, or hope, is left? What is there to work with going forward?

In the year that was 2020, and long before it was even fully fall, many looked forward to its end and to being able to say they survived it. Tee-shirts were already being printed. *I survived the year of the…*

I saw one tee-shirt that was especially apropos, although it didn't apply to any experience or year in particular: *What doesn't kill you makes you stronger. Except bears. Bears will kill you.*

The year 2020 had to be treated differently. It was like none other, after all. Sensitivity was demanded, recognition of the more than 300,000 lives lost, and counting. In too many cases, COVID-19 was like those bears. It kills. Period.

But, what about the experience of those who got sick and survived? Or those who didn't even contract the virus but survived a devastation to their finances, relationships, and more?

As we collectively fought the good fight, there was an inevitable reassessment, an accounting. There was a determination to emerge…better.

There have been other years or months or weeks or singular experiences that seemed to last forever. We didn't know if we could last another minute. We wondered if we would make it through. The takeaways are usually the same. *Well, it didn't kill me. What DID it do? Make me stronger? Wiser?*

Out of sheer exhaustion, or just thankfulness that it's over, we may just let it go. Who cares what I got out of it? There's just no time right now. I have to move on to other things, to salvage my business or get my kids caught up in school. After all, the present always comes with a myriad of new issues.

Maybe this is the time to dig a little deeper, and look again at those takeaways. Maybe we should be more intentional about insuring something positive comes out of unimaginably horrible circumstances. What a shame it would be to have gone through all that…for nothing.

* * *

Nine

What a strange number. Not even, but odd. Not a duo or trio, not ten. Not a pound or a pint or a quart. It's just *nothing* of consequence. Could it be that we haven't assigned it any significance because we're just not comfortable with it? Maybe we just can't settle into it.

When toddlers are learning to count, in any language, their goal is ten. Arriving at nine serves only as assurance that they're on the threshold, but they're not there. It means nothing.

Rob Marshall made a film called *Nine* a few years ago, but even with a stellar cast led by Daniel Day-Lewis, it was unimpressive. There was a short-lived TV series about nine survivors of a bank robbery. Not memorable. And, Jeffrey Toobin wrote a book about the Supreme Court, employing the number in its title. Good book, but it did little to lift the number to any noteworthy distinction. (And sadly, it may not be what Toobin will be remembered for.)

Gymnasts are pleased with a score of nine, but only because ten is so elusive. In fact, most anyone would be happy to achieve nine out of ten in any pursuit, but ten is still the goal. The number nine just doesn't hold any weight on its own.

There is a biblical story about Jesus healing ten people, and only one returning to thank Him. The Lord's response? *But, where are the nine?* (Luke 17:17) So, even in the Holy Scriptures, nine is associated with a pack of narcissistic ingrates. Can there be any greater reproof?

Even thirteen at least has intrigue. Nine has nothing. It's a mere vapor en route to ten. Our only conclusion can be that it is a useless, inconsequential, ugly number. But, can we live without it?

George Perec's classic novel, *A Void,* is written entirely without use of the letter *e*. The book is a mystery, a fascinating account of a group of people searching for their missing companion, with constant references to absence, loss, etc. Some among the literati have opined that the work is a metaphor for the absence of the author's parents who died in the Holocaust, i.e., the absence of an important, integral part of his life. Does this absence represent the letter *e*? I think not, because as I read, I found the story to be so masterfully written that I didn't miss the letter. I was able to live without it.

And so, as food for thought (and nothing more), I submit that we might just be able to get by without the aggravation that is the number nine.

* * *

Full

I recently arrived at one of those life decisions that are inherent with the aging process—those decisions that become necessary if we are to find any semblance of balance and peace in our lives.

I've decided I'll now need to limit the amount of information I allow into my brain.

Having always had an aversion to bureaucracy and red tape, I find lately that overly burdensome processes and requirements are too much. Not too difficult, not impossible, but just too much for my taste.

You see, I'm full. I'll need to push back from the table now, maybe take a leisurely stroll, or at least enjoy a light dessert after the heavy meal that has been life thus far. Mind you, I still have a thirst for knowledge. But I've come to the conclusion that I'll have to be a lot more selective about it.

Friends and acquaintances who are recent retirees have shared tales of misery and woe when describing the nightmare of applying for Medicare. Their stories made me dread waking up on my fast-approaching 65th birthday and lamenting the fact that I did.

As my driver's license expiration date drew near, fear and trepidation haunted me; under the federal REAL ID Act, I would apparently be required to furnish several binders full of documentation, along with my first-born child, in order to renew. I began contemplating moving to another state. Or country.

Thankfully, I learned I wouldn't have to get a REAL ID, so long as I had a current passport. With sighs of relief, even downright giddiness, I applied online to renew my regular old driver's license.

This, then, brought about a whole new concern with which to clog my brain. Why should a 60-something woman who'd had her current license for eight years, be allowed to renew it online? Shouldn't they require a new photo? A new test? How do they even know I still have all of my wits about me?

Of course this ridiculous leniency was to my advantage. I would certainly resent having to take a test and fill my brain anew with all the rules of the road. Worrying about not having to do it was a brain invasion of my own making. Let it go, girl. Just let it go.

There's a lot of information out there. Not all bad, in fact probably mostly good for personal and professional growth, etc. But the very thought of learning new procedures, filling out forms, digging up long-filed-away information and proofs and authorizations, is daunting, indeed overwhelming to me. Again, this is not about any level of difficulty. It's the level of laziness that is the problem. I just don't want to. I'm full, and I will not be force-fed any more.

Is anybody with me on this? I'm sure it's not just me.

As I flirted with the idea of retiring in another country, the notion became even more appealing as research revealed that many locations are much less complicated to call home. Even for an expat, there is so much less bureaucracy.

However, I don't believe the country alone is the problem. To an extent, life is just complicated. We're an overcrowded planet and there is a degree of bureaucracy that is necessary in order for us all to coexist.

Acknowledging that truth is going to be important for the human race. And knowing when we're full is worth considering.

* * *

Peeing on My Mom

It must have been a sunny day. A crisp, fall New Jersey afternoon, perhaps the smell of something delicious wafting from the tiny apartment's kitchen to the living room where we sat.

Of course, I had no real awareness of the sun, the meal in progress, or even the time of day. I was four, after all. The singular, keenly present truth for me at this moment, the one thing that was my whole world, was that I was sitting on my mother's lap. This was the best thing ever. In my short whisper of a lifetime, I had no memory of ever having done this before. But surely I *must* have!? No matter. This present moment was heaven, no time or space, no beginning, no end, my skinny, gangly legs dangling as I rested upon the cushiony comfort of this lap. Neither I nor my siblings counted this an especially welcoming place in our world, so the privilege was all the more delicious. Who could have known it would be *this?*

I must have squirmed a bit to get comfortable, to really settle in, but I dared not upset the apple cart too much. In the busy, hard-working reality of my parents' lives, it seemed I'd waited so very long for an inkling of a love I'd never been sure actually existed. And now, perched on this soft, ample bed of joy, I knew it was real. I also knew I had to hold on, I couldn't let it go.

There must have been some sense of what was coming. Whether I was just in denial, so desperately not wanting this snippet of pure joy to end, or whether I was so caught up in it that I really couldn't foresee what lay ahead—I did nothing to stop the train wreck.

And so it came. Before I really knew it was happening, it was. As the warm, pungent stream began to flow, my mother and I must have realized it at the same time. What was this? Where was it coming from? Me? *Was I really peeing on my mom??*

Inexplicable. No rhyme, no reason. I'd been potty trained at an early age, even started kindergarten already. I was thought of as "advanced." So, why the hell wouldn't I get up and go to the bathroom?

My last memory of the day was being urgently removed (thrown?) from the lap I so craved, as the stream of pee snaked away across the room.

* * *

An Odyssey in the Time of Corona

The Dumb and the Desperate

The dark underbelly of the physical, emotional and financial health of American seniors was brought to the fore in year 2020. A curtain was pulled back, and in too many cases what was revealed was just not a pretty picture.

Baby boomers are described as those born between 1946-1964, or age fifty-six to seventy-four as of 2020. One subset of this larger group was particularly vulnerable (and not just to the virus) in the year of COVID-19. Many late-50s and early-60s boomers found themselves in especially precarious situations. Approaching retirement, but not quite there yet; not quite enough savings; just shy of Medicare eligibility, etc. Add to that the final straw of unemployment in the year 2020.

I interviewed a number of seniors in this age group—
folks who'd reached that pre-retirement stage and
were getting serious about their final act. Not the
casual, toss-a-few-bucks-in-the-old-401K kind of
serious, but *really* serious. That's when past missteps
come back to haunt you. It's often the first time many
people realize they're not where they want to be,
where they'd hoped to be at this juncture, be it
financially, relationally, or healthwise. The only
problem is, it's too late for a do-over. Then comes a
pandemic.

What struck me as particularly sad was the self-blame
that emerged as a common thread. The sentiment
seemed to be, *We are at an age where we thought we
were pretty smart. So, why do we feel so damn dumb?
Why has regret become our middle name?*

Many wondered how they even got to this place, how
they'd allowed the missteps of life to bring them to
such abject terror when the virus began to spread.

A sad reality that became apparent during this
exercise of interviewing peers was the fact of ageism.
The treatment of our seniors in the U.S.A., especially
compared to many other countries where they are
revered and respected, is abhorrent. Of course, this
neglect was magnified during Covid. Seniors who
were infected and lost their lives were mourned of

course, but there was something almost macabre about the truths that came to light. And there was that underlying, unspoken but implied notion that they were expendable. There were even suggestions that they were *willing* to sacrifice their lives.

Then there was the reality of unemployment at age 55+. As the nationwide unemployment rate soared past ten percent, this age group was especially terrified. Their rate of joblessness was alarming long before Covid hit. Whatever the reason for the job loss, or even for those finding it necessary to re-enter the workforce after a number years, the challenges are many and the psychological and physical effects of those challenges can take a permanent toll.

Enter the desperation part. This often comes with age. If life hasn't played out the way you'd hoped, reaching boomerhood makes you keenly aware that there's less time to recover from mistakes. It's a scary place. Lonely, too, because, as some of these seniors told me, they were too ashamed to tell anyone what they were facing.

A particular challenge for this group of boomers during 2020 was the feeling of inadequacy—just one of the many side effects of ageism in any year. Some found themselves technologically challenged and unable to compete with millennials for the virtual jobs that were still available after mass layoffs and closures. Many were already experiencing being unwanted and disrespected in the workforce.

With desperation came fear. Fear of facing the uncertainty of what was happening, and of no longer having the wherewithal to be in the arena—in other words, being out of options. Their days of fighting the good fight and rising to the upper echelons (or even just surviving) in their chosen field were long behind them. The thought of accepting a lesser position at a lesser salary, or even learning a new skill, was daunting. Some just couldn't bear the reality.

In my book *A Life Alone*, I discuss the importance of introspection—taking an honest look inside and dealing with what you find. Being more agile and flexible, it's something many younger people don't yet have to confront, but during Covid seniors had to be honestly willing and able to know, accept and love themselves if they were to have a fighting chance to come out of this thing on top. There needed to be a direct corridor to the understanding that it was *not* their fault, that they were *not* dumb, and that they *could* overcome the desperation. (It may seem odd if you're facing this kind of soul-searching for the first time as a baby boomer, but it's a wonderfully cathartic exercise.)

For those who asked the question, *What will I DO?,* I could offer no immediate answers. But the door was opened for some great conversations. Well, what do you *want* to do? What are you *willing* to do?

The whole self-honesty journey might involve coming to terms with not being considered as valuable professionally as you once were, and maybe a serious pay cut. But, it's also an opportunity to give yourself a break from the rat-race of the corporate world, etc., and remove the pressure of competition with all the 30-somethings out there. Expand your horizons, and consider what *else* you might do.

Granted, these hopeful possibilities diminished somewhat once Covid darkened our doorsteps. For pre-retirement seniors, lives changed in different ways and for different reasons than the rest of the populace. But the year was a wake-up call. And we learned some things.

Ageism is a thing, and it's probably not going away any time soon. But, our years on earth are worth something. Our experience and wisdom are being put to good use by community organizations, colleges, and others. And, out of the chaos that is this virus might emerge that "final act" that we'd always wanted but never quite knew what it would look like.

Once we get intentional about not giving in to weariness or regret, our creativity and resourcefulness can kick in—and we might be surprised at the new doors that open.

Mind you, this odyssey of introspection might indeed include a stint as one of the dumb and the desperate, but it is a journey of learning and growth, and its triumphant end is in sight. Wholeness and fulfillment often come with learning things we thought we already knew, or didn't think we needed to know. (For some of us, as discussed earlier, we don't even *want* to know.) But, the result is wholeness and fulfillment nonetheless. Be courageous. Be imaginative. And, if necessary, for a time, be dumb and be desperate.

* * *

Being Me

There were not many positives to be found in Covid-19's "new normal." (Don't you just hate that phrase? I told myself I would come up with a new one, but alas…)

The eternal optimists stressed the importance of taking advantage of the quiet time afforded us by being quarantined, time to think and to read and to get back to the basics of life, as Willie and Waylon sought to do in Luckenbach, Texas. I agree that in this sense it was a rare opportunity in today's world, but I have a feeling few folks really saw it that way. Fear and uncertainty ruled the day, and it was difficult to find the positives.

For those who were able to work from home and continue receiving a full paycheck, there was the saving of gas, time and other commuting expenses, along with the cost of haircuts, makeup, and more. Not eating out and socializing was a savings as well. But for too large a percentage of the population, the cost was unbearable. The monetary cost to retailers, restaurants and their employees, and the psychological cost to some of their patrons who just never could adjust to the new void in their lives, was tremendous. Finding the good stuff in all this required an inner strength that many didn't know they had.

For unexpected reasons, some of us found our way to that positive place more quickly. I made a beeline directly to the loner in me who relished the idea of being at home for days or weeks on end, not having to muster the energy to interact with others in person, and deeply resenting it when I ran out of food or wine and had to go shopping for supplies.

But great satisfaction was derived from another surprising Covid-related circumstance. I absolutely loved wearing a mask. No, you wouldn't find me in a supermarket ranting and raving and threatening and spitting on people, knocking over displays or just generally being a jerk because someone asked me to do something that was wise, caring and respectful. On the contrary, I would have been delighted to wear the mask even if I didn't have to. For one thing, it meant I didn't have to shave my mustache. But there was another added bonus to mask-wearing, one that went much deeper.

You see, in my mask I can be me. The me who typically goes around scowling for no apparent reason, and refuses to wear a phony grin just because it's expected of me.

Now, it's not as if I'm not happy or content or thankful on any given day—it so happens that I usually am. You just wouldn't know it by looking at me. I've been told I have an RBF, something I'd never heard of before it was explained to me. I guess that just doesn't exude happiness, contentment and gratitude. On the contrary, I tend to scare little kids (just kidding). I'll never forget being told by some HR suit during an evaluation many years ago that I came across as aloof and unapproachable. This didn't surprise me, as I do own a mirror.

I can scowl at will in my mask. My b-face can be at perpetual rest, and no one is any the wiser. (Although I do have to take care to contain my struggle with eye-rolling syndrome.) I don't have to wear an insincere smile or wonder if there's spinach in my teeth from lunch. I don't have to worry about my breath, except when I just can't take it any more.

I also find the whole thing refreshing because I'm not a very trusting person, and I believe people who are *always* smiling are usually trying to sell me a bill of goods. So, masks put us all on a level playing field rather than judging one another for our respective smiles or frowns. In an effort to accentuate the positive, we can choose to look at wearing a mask as a great equalizer.

The mask I chose to wear was a bandana, that is, until it was learned that bandanas don't provide sufficient protection and I switched to a three-ply cloth mask. But I was initially amused at the notion that I probably looked more unapproachable than ever in my bandana and sunglasses, as if I was heading out to rob the stagecoach. Either way, I realized I just wasn't going to be the person others would want to approach, even at six feet. Which made me more happy, content and thankful than before. Finally, at long last, I was getting to be me.

There is something to be said for anonymity. It's a good thing when strangers don't feel as free to approach and engage. These are positives, and we should accentuate them. After all, Covid has left us with so very few.

* * *

The White Bench

I kept thinking I heard the front gate open. Each time I would drop what I was doing to go and peer out front, only to then drag my crestfallen self back to my gardening or laundry or lunch.

It's been said that once you reach a certain age, it's more difficult to find things to look forward to, and I don't disagree with that. Even the purchase of some hot new item or travel to a new destination can somehow seem old or at least comparable to something you've already purchased or seen or done. What's more, I wasn't someone who placed a lot of Amazon orders, and when I did it was almost always books. Even now, at the height of the coronavirus quarantine, there wasn't much I needed or wanted. Today was different.

Anticipation had started to build when the first text came through telling me the order would arrive today. What was this? I just didn't get this excited about anything. After all, it was just a bench for my patio. A white bench that I thought would fit perfectly into a little nook in front of a lilac tree. No big whoop. But there had to be a reason for this giddiness. Deep down, I think there must have been some notion that the nook would be a cool place for writing, and perhaps the bench held the first line to some story in the back of my mind begging to be penned. I thought about marking my calendar, for posterity's sake. White Bench Day.

It hadn't started off as my favorite day. After suffering serious shoulder pain the day before, apparently just from having slept wrong, last night I'd used a lidocaine patch. The shoulder felt better, but only slightly. I'd made some weird veggie pasta enchilada bake for breakfast, loved it but regretted the carbs, and then gone for a walk. I'd rolled my eyes at walkers not wearing masks, and come home after forty minutes. Figuring out the mystery of my dying succulents, responding to a few emails and starting the aforementioned laundry were wholly unfulfilling.

Sometimes UPS just left boxes in front of my garage and didn't even bother opening the gate or ringing the bell. In that case, my all-too-sharp-eyed neighbor would call to let me know. That is, if she'd seen the drop. I'd better check again.

While I resented the anxiety, I realized I hadn't experienced genuine excitement about anything since before the quarantine. Maybe I should revel in this a bit? Once it arrived, the possibilities would be endless. I could write. Read. Ponder things. Sit and enjoy a nice Davidoff. It would be my bench to do with as I pleased.

Another text. But it only confirmed the date, no estimated delivery time.

Just a cheap resin bench that would no doubt be a bear to put together, it would hardly be the nicest piece in my home, indoors or out. No matter. I was filled to the brim with girlish glee, and I wasn't ashamed to admit it, at least not to myself. Clearly I needed to busy myself with something, anything, before my head exploded.

There was a rewrite due in a couple of days, for an editor I'd never met but long since decided I loved because she gets me. The piece could use a little more tweaking. I was just about done with the delicious master class I'd been taking online, but wanted to look over notes from the last lesson. I was disappointed with the new instructors and classes being offered and knew I wouldn't be renewing my subscription, but I was thoroughly enjoying this last class. There was my daily Italian exercise, of course. I'd also forgotten to fill the water dish I kept on the patio for my neighbor's turtles, who wandered over periodically. (Wouldn't the bench be wonderful for turtle watching?) And, I needed to check on Celeste.

I usually started my evening workout at 5:30 just as Lester Holt began speaking, a marker signifying the winding down of my days in the time of coronavirus. With plenty of activity to fill the afternoon I should be fine until then, but—oh, my!!—what if the bench arrived in the middle of it all? Certainly I would be compelled to drop everything and tear into the treasure box. Maybe this was a time to not be so anal retentive about everything. More and more often these days, I found myself allowing my apple cart to be upset, and actually not hating it.

Another text. Arriving by 8 p.m.

Proud of the day's productivity, thankful that my sister back east was okay, I decided to polish off the roasted veggie soup I'd labored over yesterday. I'd spent a good amount of the last few weeks concocting new culinary creations, a pastime I loved. There had been a rich Cajun seafood bisque; pecan stuffed baked apples; and, when I found I was out of flour, a most unexpected oatmeal crust pizza (no, really). The last of my savory soup made me wish I'd made more.

As 7:00 p.m. approached, so too did a new dilemma. It was time for my nightly detox bath, an uninterruptable relaxation ritual that shepherded me from the confines and frustrations and anxieties of quarantine to my tranquil, fantastical place. With this bench thing, I had my own non-quarantine-related anxieties right now, so I really needed that escape. It hadn't happened in the afternoon, and time was running out. I just knew, as soon as I sank into the hot, salty water, the doorbell would ring. It shouldn't be an issue, really. So what if I retrieved the package an hour, rather than two minutes, after it arrived? Argghh!!

I took the bath, completed the sweating out of impurities, and waited. 8:05 p.m. I grabbed my phone almost violently the instant the email popped up. *We're very sorry your delivery is late. Most late packages arrive in a day. If you have not received your package by May 23, you can come back here the next day for a refund or replacement.*

Overtaken by something akin to the stages of grief, I wondered how I would even sleep. I would have to rely on the melatonin in my bath…

Day Two

No text yet. Granted, it was only 7 a.m. I'd slept, if somewhat fitfully. My morning deep breathing, reading, prayer and meditation were done, along with two cups of coffee.

I had several phone calls to make, which would allow me to walk and talk and peer out front. But then there would be the 11 a.m. Zoom meeting, chaining me to my desk, a kidnap victim of sorts.

I could only pick at the wedge salad and salmon fillet I'd chosen for lunch. It was after 12:00. Where was it? Why no updates? I couldn't take much more of this. Walking outside into the warm New Mexico sun to check on the spot I'd cleared for the new addition, I absentmindedly greeted the stealthy, thirsty turtles. The bigger one seemed to look in my direction as if to thank me for the water. A momentary, gratifying connection with a creature who knew nothing of my white bench woes. The fragrance of my jasmine plants wafted throughout the patio, their delicate white flowers crying out for a bench upon which to be properly enjoyed.

The phone startled me. Almost afraid to answer, or even look to see if I recognized the number, I tried to think quickly—something I'd never been good at. Just a bored friend whose calls had been a little more frequent than I would have preferred these last few weeks. Mindless, innocuous chit-chat that I tried to rush through without offending her. I was just too preoccupied, and by now it was getting hard to concentrate.

Two o'clock. I decided to check the tracking number, which I'd tried not to do too obsessively. Arriving by 8 p.m. Yeah, I'd heard that one before. As I brewed my afternoon cup of ginger tea, I looked at my calendar and concluded there was nothing urgent on the afternoon agenda. I would just relax. Or try to.

Settling back into my comfy Eames knockoff, I picked up the delectable old favorite that I was re-reading for maybe the fifth time in ten years. Gabriel Garcia Marquez could always provide the balm I needed in any given condition. I'd read six new books in the past few weeks, politics, poetry, fiction and more, but a re-reading of *Love in the Time of Cholera* was a no-brainer for such a time as this. As I flipped to my bookmark, I couldn't help but wonder if I would wait fifty-one years, nine months and four days for my bench.

The afternoon wore on. As I often did, I'd gotten lost in the story and allowed it to transport me to another place and time with characters who were by now old friends. But all this indulgence was depriving me of the nail-biting angst that was now my life and that I kind of liked a little.

I thought only for a second about turning on the television, but knew that on this day of all days, I didn't want to hear any updates on the virus or any of its horrific bi-products. And I could no longer stomach the contrived, feel-good coverage trying to convince us that we were all in this together.

I'd been wanting to call Eli. I longed to tell him about the bench but promised myself I wouldn't until after it was all put together and in place in its patio nook. I would send him a picture and tell him all about the last two days of hope and torture. It was hard to wait, though. Eli was the one person who would have been as excited as I was with anticipation for such a ridiculous thing. He would get it. He wouldn't ask me what it was about the bench that had my emotions in a tailspin and my stomach in knots. Eli was his own person, fascinated by other people but not concerned with what they thought about him; to my mind, a writer's writer, always a curious, quizzical look on his face (and genuine, authentic curiosity at that), always wearing his round glasses and argyle socks, even in the summer with sandals. He was the only other person I knew who was not on social media. He would commiserate but also get a kick out of my angst. I, on the other hand, wasn't getting such a kick out of it at all.

My heart leapt when the doorbell rang at 6:17 p.m.

Before taking my pocketknife to the end of the box, I stopped and did a little deep breathing. Then I went and uncorked that exquisite Malbec I'd tasted at Trader Joe's and picked up a week ago, the last time I left the house. After all, it was no longer White Bench Day. It had become a two-day affair, hence a festival. Worthy of celebration.

I realized immediately why the box was so heavy. This wasn't resin at all, but some kind of heavy metal-like vinyl with wooden braces attached to the underside of each slat. Was this even what I'd ordered? Lifting the main pieces from the box to place them in the middle of the living room, I quickly aggravated my sore shoulder. Too many parts, and inadequate instructions that included drilling a hole to connect two braces (I had no drill), might have discouraged a lesser woman. I would not be denied. I slapped on another lidocaine patch, took a sip of wine and pressed on.

It took two hours and still wasn't put together correctly. A little wobbly without the braces that required drilling, but still sturdy enough not to collapse under the weight of at least one, maybe two adults. And it looked good, so sleek and inviting. I was incredulous at how satisfying it was just to look upon. I opened both sides of the French doors leading to the patio and began dragging the thing out. It was dark now, but the solar lights were on. Pushing, pulling and inching the bench into position, I knew I had indeed chosen the right spot and measured correctly. It was perfection. I wanted to cry.

My mildly throbbing shoulder had graduated to full-blown excruciating pain, and I needed my bath. I'd left an unthinkable mess strewn across the living room floor. It was late. So, taking my Malbec and settling for the first time onto my white bench in the nook in front of the lilac tree in the time of Covid, I picked up the phone to call Eli.

* * *

But I Digress...

There came a time, after years of working as a newspaper editor, that I wanted to leave the field of journalism and explore other avenues of writing. An admitted news junkie, I decided I preferred to consume it as a leisurely pursuit, at my own pace, rather than having it force-fed to me on a daily basis and then having to regurgitate it for others' consumption.

I was already freelancing but knew I couldn't pay the bills that way. I finally settled for an offer from a non-profit to be their grant writer. That gig, although only somewhat satisfying, was doable for several years, primarily because I seemed to be good at it. Too good, apparently, as I was eventually promoted to the position of development officer (a nice name for a fundraiser who wines and dines donors, reporting to them the tremendous impact of their giving, and convincing them to give more).

It was hard to believe that an anti-social introvert could have any success at all at being winsome, outgoing and persuasive, but I seemed to be pretty effective at that, too—or at least I was good at faking it. I remained in that line of work for more than ten years, finishing out my career in a completely unexpected vocation.

I've never had even an ounce of respect for salespeople. I've always resented their patronizing, condescending way of insulting everyone's intelligence. I also never found them to be authentic. If they couldn't even convince me that *they* believed in their product, how on earth did they expect to get *me* to believe in it, let alone spend my hard-earned money for it? (Now, granted, I was generalizing, and it wasn't fair. But, when I thought of the majority of salespeople and fundraisers I'd met over the years, I just couldn't help but envision the proverbial used-car salesman with a smarmy smile, a skinny mustache and slicked-back hair.)

Once I entered that arena, I worked hard to change my views and see those in the profession as individuals. After all, I didn't want anyone to think of me that way.

No one can or should do this sort of work who doesn't believe wholeheartedly in what they are promoting. When that happens, you become an unprincipled sellout—a whore of sorts. Fortunately, I believed completely in the Christian work of my nonprofit (which I'm sure is the only reason I was successful at the job), although I didn't necessarily agree with all of its systems.

Then there was the tremendous effort it took to constantly interact with so many different people. It was draining, and over the years drove me ever-deeper into my introvert's cocoon. By then, of course, it was too late to escape the new career I'd built without even realizing it. I was old, set in my ways and too cranky and curmudgeonly to make another career change. No, I would have to wait this thing out.

Having countless conversations with countless strangers week after week is indeed exhausting, but it's also fascinating, and I was surprised to discover how many lessons could be applied to Covid quarantining once I found myself, with the rest of the world, facing this unexpected calamity.

One of the most intriguing things I learned during those years was the human tendency to diversion. If someone doesn't like the direction a dialog is taking, or just doesn't want to talk about a particular subject, even the most unskilled conversationalist has developed his or her own manner of ducking and dodging like a master. Of course, it takes a humorous turn when someone who wants something and someone who doesn't want to give it up are both engaged in trying to take a conversation in different directions. *Everyone* is an artful dodger, even those who don't know they are.

There will come parts of every journey that we simply detest, sort of like being out for a pleasant day trip and hitting the congestion of a major city's downtown traffic, right at rush hour. You can't go back. And the only way to go forward and reach your destination is to suck it up and wait it out. (At least in the privacy of your car you don't have to do it with a big, phony grin plastered on your face.) Now is the time to learn to be a formidable foe to the detours, traffic jams, and the annoying "conversations" of life. Maybe you can hop onto a surface street for awhile to make this stretch a little smoother. Perhaps pull over for a bite to eat, or just a respite to do some reading, or deep breathing. Or, just stay where you are and turn on your favorite podcast. In other words, find a way to tune out the source of the annoyance—to digress.

For many people, one of those annoyances during the pandemic became the news, local, national and international. It was all bad, and it was the source of a kind of stress we hadn't experienced before. Digression was definitely needed. In my case, I had to be intentional about limiting my consumption. I established a set time to get my updates from reliable sources, and then I let it go. (Sometimes we have to remind ourselves that we have the power to step away from the television or the newspaper—to take our day, and our stress level, in a different direction.)

Since interruptions along life's journey are inevitable, we would do well to prepare for them beforehand. We may not be able to control the offender, but we can control our reaction to it. Covid arrived as an unimaginable intrusion in all of our lives. While on its own scale of life-changing (and life-stealing) magnitude, there were some similarities to other unplanned interruptions or unpleasant conversations.

Taking control may involve some ducking and dodging, some intentional digression. Throughout our lives, we should be mindfully and intentionally practicing these skills. This will help prepare us for whatever the next stretch of road requires. Hopefully, it will involve more than just trying our hands at sourdough bread, but if that does it for you, go for it!

At the end of the day, no matter the enormity of the nightmare currently crashing into your life, be it Covid or a traffic jam, it's all about feeding your soul while biding your time—and taking control and digressing when necessary. It's the only healthy way to take the conversation in a different direction. And, as noted, we're already experts at it.

* * *

The Turning Point

There came a time in the fall that rendered me without words to describe what I was feeling. I was having a hard time identifying emotions that seemed to change by the hour.

It was two weeks before Thanksgiving. Covid numbers were skyrocketing around the nation in what was the second wave of the virus in our country. (Or third? Who knew anymore?)

I'd just returned from my first business trip in eight months, having visited three different states and experienced a headspinning variety of restrictions, violations and hostilities.

A typical return from a work trip involved being happy to be home combined with the satisfaction of productive meetings and an overall successful trip. This was not that.

Settling in to begin my mandatory 14-day quarantine, I was filled with regret at having gone and, for the first time, concern that I might have been exposed. Processing these brand-new sentiments was only the beginning.

By day five after my return home I started to relax a bit, even though it was still early in the incubation period. That same day the governor held a presser that hit like a ton of bricks. While our state had boasted some of the best containment stats in the nation throughout the summer due to a partial shutdown, reopening in phases, and the vigilance of our citizenry, all that had now changed drastically.

It felt different this time, dire, like a grim turning point. I wondered if anyone else was receiving this news the way I was. Maybe it was just me, but I suddenly knew that serious changes were in order.

I ordered my groceries online for the first time that weekend, and scheduled curbside pickup. (Although tempting, I'd resisted this move all year, no doubt a control issue.) Beyond that, the decision was made not to leave the house, at least until I could put a label on what I was feeling.

I'd always been one of the good ones, wearing my mask faithfully, social distancing, hand-washing, staying home. None of it had been an imposition, but rather came so very naturally. I prayed for those who struggled with the restrictions. Many had flat-out refused, even rebelled, demanding their freedom (to die? to kill others?), but I did understand how difficult it all was for the social butterflies, the conspiracy theorists and the downright stupid.

While I'd done my best to obey the new rules right along, now I felt it hadn't been enough. All of the good guys' efforts could not overcome the rebels' irresponsible antics.

Certainly it wasn't just now becoming serious. I'd always taken it seriously. So, why did it suddenly seem so much more unnerving? And where to go from here? What do I do with this? These new emotions for which I had no descriptors?

News reports featured tired anchors with their doctor guests warning all of us to stay home for Thanksgiving, and then cutting to scenes of crowded airports as everyone promptly ignored them. *Nothing can stop me from being with my family,* remarked one jovial traveler to the camera. Oh, yes. Something could.

I was thankful when my office announced a new closure, everyone to work from home for at least the next two weeks, which would later be extended. I wouldn't have to go in after my quarantine ended.

Day fourteen brought overwhelming gratitude. But there was still that nagging foreboding. Numbers were through the roof nationwide. The political situation was chaotic, the product of someone's alternate-universe thinking; and my 16-year-old granddaughter tested positive.

Her symptoms were mild, but my son had to leave the house temporarily due to an existing condition, leaving my daughter-in-law at increased risk while caring for the home and their two girls. The helplessness and frustration were now all-consuming.

After ten days they all tested negative, my son returned to his family, and we had the difficult phone conversation to plan for the holidays. Thanksgiving was out, of course. They wanted to drive up from Phoenix for Christmas and we nervously, tentatively penciled it in. I doubted it would happen.

I hung in there, staying busy with work, checking periodically on friends and family, reading, inventing recipes and sticking to my vow to work out every day (well, almost). But deep down I still knew this was different.

Still not willing to call it fear, words continued to fail me. I decided to stop searching, but I did settle on a couple. Perhaps not yet panic, but certainly urgency. And not so much at the impending doom of Covid during the approaching winter months, but the total and complete ignorance of my fellow man. This was madness.

* * *

American Politics: An Odyssey of Race, Religion and Rancor

Asphyxia

I awoke last night to a panic attack—heart pounding, out of breath, tears streaming down my face. I thought I'd had a nightmare, of being in a car accident. Then I realized it wasn't a dream at all, but the continuation of an ongoing reality. There had indeed been yet another horrific crash in this never-ending pileup, and its name was George Floyd. Now, the victimization was coming to fruition.

In late 2019, I decided to retire in Sicily. I'd been toying with the notion of retiring to a faraway place for years, but now it was a concrete decision. As a lover of southern Italy, it wasn't a difficult one, especially when the region started offering those cheap homes to anyone willing to renovate them.

My target date was 2021, and even after Covid-19 hit, I was not deterred.

Now I began to wonder if I could wait that long. The need to get out of my country was suddenly overwhelming. This notwithstanding the thankfulness I hold for the privilege of calling the U.S.A. my home, particularly after spending years in developing countries around the world. At this moment, I would feel safer in any one of those nations.

It's this multi-car pileup that is igniting the urgency. Having been thrown violently from the belted security of my driver's seat, where I'd allowed myself to feel safe despite knowing the inevitable dangers that lurked, I now lie crumpled on the sweltering blacktop, bleeding, terrified, needing to somehow extricate myself from the tangled mass of vehicles. I am in the midst of it, surrounded by it, and I am suffocating. But for now I can only lie here, waiting for someone to pull me from the wreckage. Clearly, no one is coming.

For a moment I'd foolishly allowed myself to believe the last crash was truly the final one, and we were now in the aftermath of it all. There were already so many vehicles, after all. But no, this accident, so calculated and deliberate, is ongoing. It is a pileup of unfathomable proportion, with no end in sight.

As I lie here I notice that with each screeching of brakes and deafening crash, one into another then another, there seems to be less panic on the part of the oncoming drivers, even after they realize what is about to happen. Now, they're hardly even applying brakes at all, not even with the awareness of being caught on camera. No concern about receiving that citation in the mail or their insurance premiums increasing, no fear of being injured themselves once the final strike brings about the inevitable result of their recklessness.

I want to cry out, to jump in front of one of the oncoming vehicles and stop them before it's too late. But alas, I cannot stand. Or even move. I have no voice. I am powerless, lying here with my silent screams. I am suffocating.

When will rescue arrive? Has anyone even called? Squinting my eyes to see yet another driver approaching at a speed that will render him unable to stop in time, I realize he *is* the cavalry. Or at least he's supposed to be. Is there no one else? No other hope?

Casualties are mounting. I can no longer watch. I must find a way to drag myself out of here. I am suffocating.

Bystanders, witnesses, relatives, and members of black and brown communities throughout this nation are victims of this ongoing horror. Surviving victims, but victims nonetheless. We remain in the land of the living, mourning our losses, battered, weak, and weary, waiting in terror for the next strike. The burden is tremendous. Helpless ourselves, do we abandon the equally defenseless and find a way to flee, or force ourselves to stay and watch the carnage, wondering who will be next?

As the mother of a black man in America, I am grieved. I am afraid, and so very tired. But I am torn. Do I leave, knowing the dangers he faces each day of his life just because of who he is? Or do I stay, knowing there is not one thing I can do to help him should he stumble unawares upon the massive crash up ahead? Even if he avoids the pileup, he could so easily fall victim to a privileged dog walker putting his life at risk with a phone call. I am not sure I can bear to leave him, but certain I cannot bear to stay.

What once was a carefree dalliance with the idea of moving to another country has now become a desperate exigence. I am suffocating. After nearly 50 years in the workforce, a tax-paying, home-owning, law-abiding citizen of this land of the free, my land, I still cannot hope to retire in peace—and breathe.

* * *

Fixing Us

There are a number of efforts afoot in today's volatile cultural climate to correct social ills that have plagued our society from its beginning. Many of these efforts are rushed, almost desperate, and at the end of the day amount to little more than guilt-appeasing stopgap measures with no lasting effect. Social service at times obscures the need for social justice by confusing compassion (whether real or feigned) with change. As Dr. Martin Luther King, Jr. said, charity is a poor substitute for justice.

In response to my remarks about certain current injustices during an informal gathering of churchgoers, one man commented that "there are a lot of hurting hearts that we need to minister to." *No, my friend,* I thought (but didn't say), *I don't need you to minister to me after you've brutalized me. I need you to stop brutalizing me. Your brand of ministry is far too often just a superficial attempt to assuage your sense of guilt or to keep up appearances. It is a band-aid on a cancerous tumor.*

Sadly, much of the aforementioned "ministry" often amounts to advice as to how others should live, speak, respond—all according to what the adviser deems appropriate. Most appalling are attempts to "remake" black and brown Americans under the guise of social service or some sort of perceived allyship, in order to prevent us from being brutalized. This, rather than prevent the brutalizers from committing their heinous acts.

If only he hadn't run…worn that hoodie…acted so suspicious…jogged in that neighborhood…gone to sleep in her own home.

I liken certain white evangelical attempts to "fix" us to a smoky room full of male legislators making decisions about female healthcare, or American and British missionaries going into African, Asian and Latin American countries to teach people how to be people. This is a classic faux pas among missionaries whose mandate is to serve, and to provide information, i.e., tell people about their God, not to disrespect and denigrate people's culture, or attempt to turn people into "civilized" Americans or Brits. Missionaries charged with providing medical care, etc., are often guilty of treating adult patients as one would a child or a pet.

The whole providing of information thing is a problem in itself, harking back to the long-accepted but vehemently denied practice on the part of white America to deny others access to equal education. "Equal" is the operative term here. It should not be up to one group to decide how much or what type of education is available to another group. The old "teach a man to fish" adage is an example of such presumptive superiority. It is flawed partly because, in truth, most people don't need to be taught to fish. They simply need access to the lake.

One possible challenge to efforts toward equality is that some folks believe being *equal* to them means being *like* them—doing things their way, thinking like them, finding life's enjoyment and fulfillment in the same things. This is problematic because it denotes an intrinsic disregard and disrespect for the qualities, mannerisms, likes and dislikes of others who are not like them.

There is also the existential threat represented in "otherdom." A number of evangelical Christians, as well as many American whites from all walks and belief systems, live in a parallel universe in which truth threatens their utopia. They grapple with whether others should be allowed to be themselves, lest they take over. Or, God forbid, the others might be better, smarter, or....naahh, can't be. Let's not go crazy here. Everyone knows the others are inherently inferior, intellectually and in every way. The only thing to do is keep trying to fix them.

Global warming, racial intellectual equality, white privilege, etc., are all truths that are simply denied by many white evangelicals. Likewise, the fact that not all "good" Christians are Republicans, and vice versa, are concepts that many simply cannot fathom. So, when a Republican shows him or herself to be an un-Christlike, immoral n'er-do-well beyond their justification, they are forced to turn a blind eye. The only alternative would be to face truth.

One of the reasons for this self-imposed dilemma is the aforementioned utopia. In the view of many in this wing of evangelicalism, anything that they deem bad or problematic is due to sin, but the sin of others, not themselves. Or, they will simply deny the problem exists at all, attributing any talk of it to fake news.

Such willful blindness is, in part, what leads to an insistence that the solution to all of our problems can only be found in simply obeying the Commandments, keeping a low profile and our mouths shut. This in spite of the fact that we have a flawed justice system that lies at the heart of so many of those ills. But no, the answer is not to change that system, but to change *us*. To fix us. Because clearly, we're the broken ones.

* * *

The Big Picture

Esther is a petite, short-haired woman with a youthful vigor that belies her 75 years. Her pale, leathery skin burns easily when walking about the Southern California citrus groves that she's run singlehandedly since buying the farm on a whim 40 years earlier, after a corporate career in downtown Chicago. She's never married. A strong, independent thinker, a formidable woman to be sure.

During a conversation at the height of the coronavirus outbreak in the U.S., Esther remarked how very thankful she was that we have a Christian president to lead us through the crisis. Curious to understand her thinking, I proffered that many people say they're Christians when it's convenient, but they don't walk the walk (or, in biblical terms, "bear fruit," which is how we're supposed to recognize a Christian in the first place). I waited for the defense. Radio silence. Somehow, she is at once a devout Christian and a diehard supporter of 45, but unable (or unwilling) to offer any explanation for the seeming dichotomy.

For many Americans, this remains an inexplicable contradiction, a mystery that cannot be solved. Some have given up trying. But, in the summer of 2020, in an effort to make more sense of the coming election than could be made of 2016, others doggedly pressed on. Some felt forced to defend their Christian faith against the negative labels and judgments now associated with the current President. Others just felt forgotten and cast aside. Wanting no parts of an association with this POTUS, they were resentful that their Christianity had been hijacked and lumped together with the majority of the white evangelical community.

And then there are, and always will be, the Esthers. How did we get here?

Most of us will never forget the start of the 2008 presidential election. The early announcements back in '07. The first tenuous steps into campaign season. And the one glaring anomaly that made it unlike any American election there had ever been.

The level of the vitriol and division that followed right through that groundbreaking campaign and the ensuing eight years had not been seen since the civil rights era, maybe even as far back as the Civil War.

I was (and remain) of the mind that the foundation for much of the hostility was race. Many disagree. But, the debate that began all those years ago has not abated even in the aftermath of that eight-year presidency. Far from it. The rage, bitterness and resentment have only increased. In what might be seen as an overcorrection, the 2016 election was equally groundbreaking, adding nuances that gobsmacked journalists, politicians and historians still furiously explore and debate. One of the foremost of those nuances is, of course, the element of religion. Or, more specifically, evangelical Christianity.

The fundamental, mind-bending question of how on earth one can call oneself a Christian, with the moral and ethical responsibility that that entails, and yet still have helped to bring about the political condition that began in 2016, may never be satisfactorily answered. In his National Review article entitled *Understanding Why Religious Conservatives Would Vote for Trump* (February 10, 2020), Andrew T. Walker attempts an explanation:

> *...blind allegiance does not explain the voting relationship. That religious conservatives are not progressives does. Between Never Trump and Always Trump is a third category: Reluctant Trump. Voters in this category don't get the fair hearing they deserve, since they defy the simple binary portrayal of religious conservatives as either offended by Trump or sold out to him.*

One might argue that the evangelicals whose moral convictions preclude them from voting for blatant immorality, who are largely Christian voters of color, also don't get the fair hearing they deserve. The "Christian right," and even Christians in general, are often unfairly categorized under one banner for political and journalistic convenience: white evangelicals.

Walker contends that those reluctant supporters are able to see past the uncouth, the immoral, even the corrupt, to focus on the one or two issues that they believe can make or break our democracy. And, more importantly, issues that are at the core of their Christian faith. Referencing the President's call for banning late-term abortion during his last State of the Union address, "as Democrats sat stone-faced," Walker wrote:

A moment of such moral contrast demonstrates why religious conservatives do not care about the endless think pieces criticizing them as soulless hypocrites. They will endure that criticism if it means the chance to end abortion through Supreme Court appointments. To the average religious conservative (like me), there is no moral ambiguity about abortion. It must be stopped. It's a morally transcendent issue.

Citing Beto O'Rourke's proclamation during a 2019 town hall that churches not supporting transgender rights would lose their tax-exempt status under his administration, Walker said religious conservatives saw this as a pivotal moment, a turning point calling all true believers to step up and fight the good fight in the voting booth. His representation of this faction of religious conservatives portrayed a careful, thoughtful, faithful band that has its priorities in order. His piece offered an explanation, not a defense, because this is a group that doesn't feel it needs defending. Personally, I appreciated that there at least *was* an explanation, if only for a small number of the ardent supporters that effected the 2016 victory.

Another of the primary passions of the voting believer is science. For some, the election was reduced to science vs. Christianity. But are the two really mutually exclusive? An honest reckoning might reveal otherwise.

Scripture tells us that *Every good and perfect gift is from above...* (James 1:17). Aren't medical technology and our amazing scientific advances good and perfect gifts? Could it be that what we're really grappling with is how we've chosen to use those gifts, rather than the perceived evil of the gifts themselves?

Artistic beauty is another God-given gift. But, what the world sees as art is sometimes appalling to many Christians. Beauty is in the eye of the beholder, and personal preferences are indeed shaped by our Christian foundation or lack of same. None of that changes the original gift or the intent of the Giver. To apply such narrow thinking to anything that is of God is to minimize the magnitude of His glory, His holiness, His sovereignty.

We tend to exist today in miniscule bubbles of our own making and our own limited understanding. We've even denied ourselves the wide expanse of gifts and information God has made available to us, to equip us to make balanced, informed choices. Are we forgetting His omniscience? Are we choosing to deny it, believing that we somehow know better?

As Christians, perhaps we would do well in our decision-making to step back and take a broader view…God's view. In our politics, on what do we base our judgments? On ourselves? On one another? The Bible says, *When they measure themselves by themselves and compare themselves with themselves, they are not wise.* (2 Corinthians 10:12). Ought not we to pray for expanded horizons, deeper understanding?

If narrow criteria are to be applied to the Christian vote, such criteria must not be personal but rather those given us by God. The Ten Commandments. The Sermon on the Mount. These parameters would have precluded the overwhelming Christian support of Donald Trump for the U.S. presidency in 2016 and again in 2020.

Okay, so the one-issue voter is explanation number one, but it only accounts for some of the Christian electorate. What about the rest? One still cannot help but marvel at those religious conservatives who are not reluctant supporters but enthusiastic zealots who truly believe the man himself, not any particular issue, is the Chosen One. (And while we're here, let's put to rest the notion that he is or ever was a "baby Christian" slowly but determinedly gaining his footing in the faith. This simply strains credulity, given his continued abhorrent words and actions.)

The contortionists that many have become in an effort to defend the indefensible, minus allegiance to any weighty spiritual issue, cannot be explained. The most vulgar conduct, filthiest language, grossest lies, blatant racism, vicious and unfounded attacks are dismissed as "misbehavior," or "indelicate speech," or "eccentricities." In some cases, 45's base just seemed to resort to plugging their ears and refusing to hear. La la la la la la la…..

For a large contingent of these voters, the only issue is the party itself. They offer explanation number two, the belief that Republican and Christian are synonymous. A blind allegiance to a party is misguided, yes, but there it is. Once again, at least it provides some basis for an otherwise incomprehensible stance. In a May 2016 paper for Oxford Research Encyclopedias entitled *Party Identification and Its Implications,* author Russell J. Dalton suggests:

> *Early electoral research in the United States discovered the most important concept in the study of political behavior:*

party identification. Party identification is a long-term, affective attachment to one's preferred political party. Cross-national research finds that these party identities are a potent cue in guiding the attitudes and behavior of the average person. Partisans tend to repeatedly support their preferred party, even when the candidates and the issues change. Party ties mobilize people to vote to support their party, and to work for the party during the campaign. And given the limited information most people have about complex political issues, party ties provide a cue to what positions one should support.

Got it. There's loyalty to an issue and loyalty to a party. What remains unexplained is the devotion to the individual, and the blind acceptance of the "he's a Christian" argument in the face of overwhelming evidence to the contrary.

Not one of us is in a position to judge another's Christianity. But we are called to exercise God-given wisdom before hopping aboard anyone's bandwagon, whether that person is a believer or not. In fact, we're directed explicitly not to become followers of certain types. And yes, we do know them by their fruit.

There is a possible explanation number three. A candidate who is shown to be far and away above his or her opponents in experience, intellect, competence, expertise in constitutional law and international relations, might be a no-brainer nominee. However, this is not that, and one might be hard-pressed to identify even a small fraction of voters who hold this stance in the case before us today.

If in fact the primary issue is abortion, in accordance with these voters' Christian faith, or simply an adherence to anything and everything Republican, then why not nominate a lifelong Republican; why not a *true* Christian whose anti-abortion views are based on his or her faith rather than the direction of current political winds? There were a number of Republican candidates from which to choose in 2016, some of whom had professed and lived out their Christian faith throughout their public lives.

The 39th president of the United States, Jimmy Carter, has taught Sunday School at Maranatha Baptist Church, in his hometown of Plains, Georgia, for decades. But, long before that, he taught Bible study at Annapolis when he was a midshipman, and even on occasion during his presidency. Although the church's membership is less than 50, visitors who flock to Maranatha Baptist when Carter is teaching number in the hundreds on any given Sunday. They come from far and wide, and they run the gamut from conservative Republicans from the deep south to big city liberals from Chicago. They know Carter's lesson will be about Jesus Christ, not himself and not politics. Like the teacher, they have their priorities in order.

(Interestingly, Maranatha Baptist Church is the product of a church split back in the seventies. When the original church would not allow black people to join, some of its members left and formed Maranatha. The Christian principle of impartiality was that important to them. The current pastor is Maranatha's first black pastor.)

The story of Jimmy Carter living his faith out loud is the stuff of legend. For example, he was once laughed to scorn for publicly confessing the sin of "lusting in his heart." This all begs the question whether there were Republicans who voted for the Democrat Carter because he was a Christian, or who voted against him simply because he was a Democrat.

One glaring element to the mystery before us as we tried to figure things out in 2020 was the overwhelming whiteness of the 2016 voters in question. Comparable numbers of black Christians are anti-abortion and anti-LGBTQ, citing their faith as the inarguable basis for their stance. This group is equally careful, thoughtful and faithful. And yet, their vote in large majority would never support 45 as POTUS. Hmmm...could it possibly be that part of the foundation of this divide is also race? Let's put a pin in that one.

Many Christians not only believe abortion and homosexuality are sin, but that they are the "big ones," the most egregious to a holy God. There is Scripture to support the opposing view that God sees all sin the same. James 2:10 says, *For whosoever shall keep the whole law, and yet offend in one point, he is guilty of all.* Liars, haters, gossips and cheats don't like that one. And, of course Scripture can easily be found to dispute that view. Much too often, particularly in these contentious times, the Bible is taken out of context, with various Old and New Testament passages randomly tossed about to suit the occasion. Interpretations vary widely.

A number of non-believers invoke the separation of church and state to counter Christians whose faith is their foundation for anti-abortion and anti-LGBTQ views. Some Christians, on the other hand, feel these issues are the crux of our democracy, as outlined in the Walker piece. (It is noteworthy that the latter group also believes in large part that the U.S. is a Christian country that was founded as such and must be preserved as such.)

Noted journalist and historian Jon Meacham posits another approach for applying Christian faith in accomplishing our civic duty. In a February 2020 New York Times op-ed entitled *Why Religion Is the Best Hope Against Trump,* marking the start of the Lenten season, Meacham writes:

> *For many Americans, especially non-Christians, the thought that Christian morality is a useful guide to much of anything these days is risible, particularly since so many evangelicals have thrown in their lot with a relentlessly solipsistic American president who bullies, boasts and sneers. The political hero of the Christian right of 2020 has used the National Prayer Breakfast to mock the New Testament injunction to love one's enemies, and it's clear that leading conservative Christian voices are putting the Supreme Court ahead of the Sermon on the Mount. And yet history suggests that religiously inspired activism may hold the best hope for those in*

> *resistance to the prevailing Trumpian order.*

Quoting the words of the Rev. Dr. Martin Luther King Jr., in a passage inspired by theologian Walter Rauschenbusch, Meacham continues:

> *The Gospel at its best deals with the whole man, not only his soul but his body, not only his spiritual well-being, but his material well-being. Any religion that professes to be concerned about the souls of men and is not concerned about the slums that damn them, the economic conditions that strangle them and the social conditions that cripple them is a spiritually moribund religion awaiting burial.*

For some, then, the focus must be broader than one issue, notwithstanding that issue's tremendous gravity and influence on our national condition. There must be more of a big-picture approach. In discussing the notion of some Christians that there is only one way to achieve their desired goals (i.e., vote Republican, no matter the candidate), Meacham said, *The American past unmistakably tells us that one way to a more perfect union, one way to a nation where equality before the law and before God is more universal, is the way of Dr. King. Which is also the way of Jesus.*

The inability, or flat refusal, to see the big picture comes with unnecessary risk. As Covid-19 heated up across the country, state after state implemented some measure of a stay-at-home order. Nonessential businesses closed. Gatherings of more than five people were prohibited, mask-wearing was mandatory and social distancing of six feet was the order of the day. But several churches defied these mandates and continued to hold in-person services. A couple of pastors were arrested, and seemed to relish the opportunity to speak publicly about their faith in a healing God who would protect true believers from the virus.

Faith is a wonderful thing. How we choose to exercise it can be problematic. I'm reminded of the old joke about the guy who was stranded on the roof of his home in a flood. A group of rescuers comes by in a rowboat and urges him to get in. "No thanks, God's gonna save me," he responds cheerfully. As the waters rise, along comes another boat, this one with a couple of neighbors. "I'm okay," he assures them, "God's gonna save me." Taking his word for it, they move on. Next comes a helicopter, lowering a rope ladder to the man. He refuses. Long story short, our faithful friend drowns and goes to heaven. "Why didn't you save me?" he asks the Lord. "Well, I sent you two boats and helicopter," says God.

Faith without works is dead. James 2:17.

God has not only given us faith, but wisdom. We're expected to exercise both, and act accordingly. A healthy dose of common sense might well put to rest much of the conflict and partisanship that plague us today. We will never have all the answers, but wisdom demands that we not blindly and thoughtlessly hitch our wagon to a fallible human being whose particular fatal flaws are on full display and dictate his actions. Faith and party affiliation notwithstanding, we would do well to simply *think*—to consider rationally what we have before us. Perhaps take a step back and consider matters from a better vantage point. A big picture perspective.

Justice is supposed to be blind. Its keepers, charged with doling it out, and their followers, are not supposed to be. As Meacham reflects in his 2020 book of Holy Week meditations entitled *The Hope of Glory,*

> *History and theology are inextricably bound up with each other…together, they create truth. Fact is what we can see or*

161

discern; truth is the larger significance we extrapolate from those facts.

By the time the long summer of 2020 faded and the campaign season drew mercifully to a close, I'd queried Christians of all stripes. Many adhered to at least one of the concepts discussed here, in some form or other. There were also outliers, clinging to far-flung notions based on faulty data. Folks were all over the map; there was to be no harmony, no majority opinion. And, within the Christian voting bloc, one was hard-pressed to find God in the mix.

It took five days until we knew. Five days of acrimony, rancor, and all manner of ridiculousness. Post-election interviews depicted many evangelicals lamenting the nation's sure destruction under the new administration, all the while ignoring the destruction already in progress under the current one. True to form, the facts would do little to alter the views of those die-hards. Their magical thinking allowed them to join the ranks of deniers and conspiracy theorists. Their one-issue passions, party loyalty and willful blindness simply would not permit conciliation.

In the end, the dear leader was dethroned, the correction completed, despite bizarre and laughable legal efforts to overturn the results and deny the will of the majority. Our long national nightmare had ended. Would another one begin? A seriously divided country, brimming with Christians, held its collective breath.

* * *